Grow a Family Tree!

Grow a Family Tree!

Seven Simple Steps

by William Dollarhide

HeritageQuest®
From ProQuest Company
North Salt Lake, Utah
2000

Other Books
by William Dollarhide

Published by Genealogical Publishing Co., Inc., Baltimore, Maryland:

- *Map Guide to the U.S. Federal Censuses, 1790-1920*
  (with William Thorndale) (1987)

- *Managing a Genealogical Project* (rev. 1998)

- *Genealogy Starter Kit* (rev. 1998)

Published by Heritage Quest, North Salt Lake, Utah:

- *Map Guide to American Migration Routes, 1735-1815* (1997)

- *British Origins of American Colonists, 1629-1775* (1997)

- *America's Best Genealogy Resource Centers*
  (with Ronald A. Bremer) (1998)

- *The Census Book: A Genealogist's Guide to Federal Census
  Facts, Schedules, and Indexes* (1999)

Contents

Table of Contents

Preface

Like most genealogists, I believe that my ancestors were so interesting that I often share with other people the wonderful stories I have discovered. For some reason, not everyone seems as interested as me.

On the other hand, when people insist on telling me the long, boring details of their genealogy, I find it very hard to stay awake.

Genealogy Rule #1:
I'm crazy about genealogy, but not necessarily yours!

A family history, it seems, is a fascinating subject, but only when it applies to your own ancestors. But, genealogy has become a very popular hobby in America because the discovery of our roots is a personal and rewarding experience, even if we do have trouble getting people to listen to us.

Now It's Your Turn!

You were born with an interest in your family origins, but for years you resisted the urge to do much about it. But now, as a baby boomer, you have reached the age when you are required to do something about it; and you wonder if this book will help.

Grow a Family Tree! begins as a basic training manual for the study of family origins. The first part of this book is presented as a sequence of steps that can be followed in the discovery of your ancestors. Along the way, several different types of resources may be involved; but the basic steps will not change. And, the sequence may be repeated after previously unknown ancestors are identified. The purpose is to provide baby boomers (or their children or parents) the tried and true steps that can be used to grow a family tree.

Genealogy Rule #2:
Don't put the hearse before the horse.

In the second part of the book, there are several essays explaining the most important aspects of genealogical research, including examples and case studies, all taken from articles written by the author for the Genealogy Bulletin over the past few years.

The third part of the book includes some research forms designed for making copies.

To help you get through the time you will need to read this book, there are several Genealogy Rules (like the two on this page) and a few cartoons have been interspersed throughout the text.

I invite you to read on and start growing your own family tree. But whatever you do, don't tell anyone!

— William Dollarhide

All I did was go on the Internet and ask for a printout of the Johnson Family !

Preface

Part I
How to Grow a Family Tree

What are the Steps?

There is a sequence of repeatable steps that can be followed in genealogical research. The seven steps are identified in this section. They are as follows:

Step 1 — Do Your Homework. Everything starts with the collection of information about your family from sources found at home.

Step 2 — Start Family Sheets. A family group sheet is a basic tool for recording genealogical information. Creating family sheets is the way you learn what you know and what you don't know and will help you organize the project.

Step 3 — Locate More Relatives. Since your relatives may be the best sources for genealogical information, they need to be contacted. We include many tips for finding lost relatives.

Step 4 — Get the Vital Records. Vital records may provide the first written proof of a person's existence and need to be obtained for anyone closely related.

Step 5 — Search the Census Records. Federal censuses taken since 1790 provide a place to find an ancestor's name, as well as family information. Censuses are best for finding the place where a person lived back in time and may be the first resources that will give genealogical success.

Step 6 — Survey the Local and State Resources. Perhaps the best place to find genealogical references to a person is in a local courthouse or other facility near the place a person lived. Once a place of residence for an ancestor is known, these records need to be identified for their genealogical value.

Step 7 — Survey the National Resources. Resources located at the National Archives provide a place to find solid evidence of an ancestor's life.

Trial Pedigree Chart

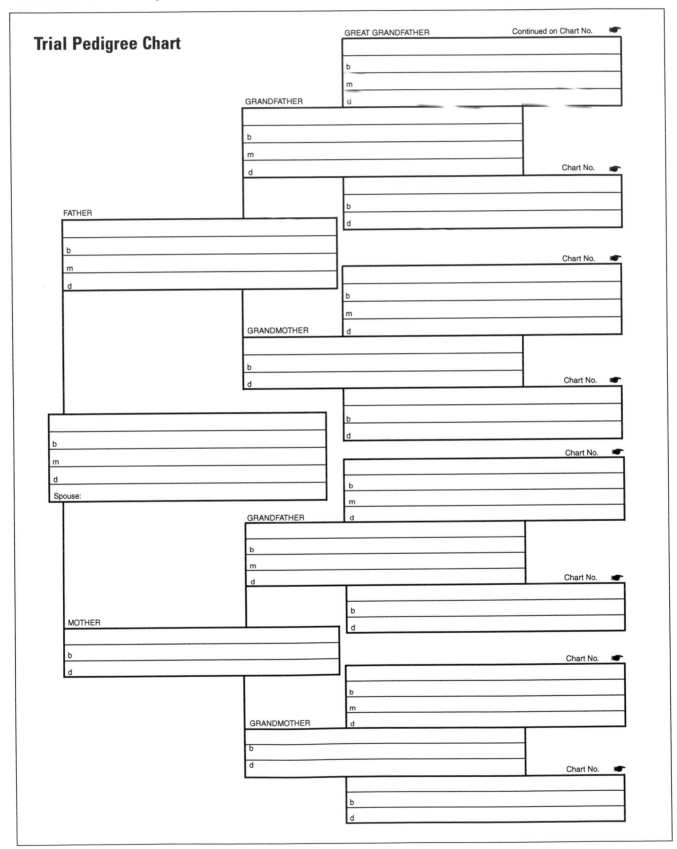

Do Your Homework

Genealogy Rule No. 3: **Get a life! Then write it!**

Start a Pedigree Chart

One way to quickly learn what you don't know about your ancestors is try to fill out a pedigree chart. A **pedigree** is a diagram that identifies the direct ancestors for a person, that is, their parents, grandparents, great-grandparents, and so on.

On the opposite page is a trial pedigree chart. Use the chart as a test to determine what you know. From your memory only, fill in as much as you can about yourself and your immediate ancestors. Every blank or incomplete name, date, or place, will indicate where you need to start in the discovery of your ancestry. If you are able to fill in the complete pedigree chart through yourself, parents, grandparents, and great-grandparents, you probably don't need this book! But if every space is not filled in, then you have work to do.

The blanks on the chart should suggest some questions, such as "Who knows this stuff?" or "Do I know where I can find this information?" or even, "What am I getting into here?"

Taking Stock

With the incomplete pedigree chart as a guide, the discovery process begins. The process starts at home. Start by taking stock of what family information you may have at home. You are looking for anything that might mention names, dates, or places of residence for people in your family. These could be old photo albums, newspaper clippings, or anything else that may contain genealogical information. You may find birth or death certificates for members of your family. But, you may also find insurance papers, a family Bible, baby books, anniversary books, greeting cards, or old letters. In this search, you need to think of items which give names, dates, places, and other facts about the family. Here is a list of items that could be in your home, and if so, a place where genealogical information may be found.

Checklist of Home Sources:

- ☐ Adoption records
- ☐ Anniversary guest books
- ☐ Automobile insurance papers
- ☐ Baby announcements
- ☐ Baby books
- ☐ Baptism records
- ☐ Citizenship papers
- ☐ Confirmation records
- ☐ Credit statements
- ☐ Death announcements
- ☐ Death certificates
- ☐ Diaries and journals
- ☐ Diplomas
- ☐ Discharge papers
- ☐ Divorce papers
- ☐ Draft cards
- ☐ Driver's licenses
- ☐ Employment records
- ☐ Family Bibles
- ☐ Family business papers
- ☐ Family correspondence
- ☐ Family pictures
- ☐ Family histories
- ☐ Family needlepoint
- ☐ Fire insurance papers
- ☐ Funeral programs
- ☐ Graduation records
- ☐ Health insurance cards
- ☐ Income tax forms
- ☐ Land deeds
- ☐ Life insurance papers
- ☐ Magazine subscriptions
- ☐ Marriage certificates
- ☐ Military records
- ☐ Motor vehicle registrations
- ☐ Naturalization papers
- ☐ Newspaper clippings
- ☐ Newspaper obituaries
- ☐ Oral histories
- ☐ Photo albums
- ☐ Prepared ahnentafels
- ☐ Prepared descendancies
- ☐ Prepared pedigrees
- ☐ Probate/estate records
- ☐ Property tax records
- ☐ Report cards
- ☐ School enrollments
- ☐ Scrapbooks
- ☐ Social security cards
- ☐ Union cards
- ☐ Wedding announcements
- ☐ Wedding guest books

This inventory work could make you the hero of your family if you tell everyone that they don't have to keep track of anything, just help you find stuff. Promise everyone that you will give them all a copy of "the book" you will be doing on the family. Lying to your family is permitted in this phase.

Genealogy Rule No. 4:
With any luck, some of the people in your family could read and write . . . and may have left something written about themselves.

Recording Memories

Unless you have the ability to communicate with the dead, you need to interview your living relatives. This includes your parents, grandparents, brothers, sisters, and any other close relatives. These interviews are part of the inventory, because you need to collect all of the information about your ancestry from the sources at home. But, the first person you need to interview is yourself.

If some important official (like a clerk at a convenience store) asks you for your identification, how do you respond? You would probably produce some document to prove your identity, such as a driver's license. You often have to produce photo-ID before cashing checks or after being stopped for going 85 in a 35 mph speed zone. But aside from the ID you carry on you, what other document can you produce that proves who you really are? For example, do you have a copy of your own birth certificate? What other written document can you think of that identifies you?

Most of us have more of the personal facts about ourselves in our heads, not on paper. But to get prepared and begin the process of discovery of your ancestors, you need to gather the facts that may reside only in your memory, just as though they were documents residing in a courthouse. In other words, you have to write the stuff down! In genealogy, you need to obtain documents that prove what you say about yourself is true. More importantly, you need to collect these documents for each person in your pedigree. To do this, you should first collect the information that exists in your memory by writing it on paper.

Create a Database

As a new genealogist, you will become a collector of notes and documents. Your written family history will not become a reality until you collect enough of these notes and documents, and a family history emerges. In order to collect these documents, you need to be a sleuth. You need to turn yourself into a detective and ask questions about your life and the lives of your ancestors. You need to create a **database** of information composed of facts you gather from your memory as notes, as well as the written documents. The database contains the facts about your ancestors and will be used to compile written reports about individuals, families, and lineages.

What is in your memory can not be in the database until it is written down. How you write it doesn't matter. A plain sheet of paper with a title, "What I remember about Dad" is enough. Now you can write what you remember about his birth, marriage, death, and anything else. When you have finished writing, you have created a document. That document has the same value as a legal document obtained from a courthouse!

Use the same method when you interview other members of your family. Take notes! The notes can be specific to one person. Start the page with something like, "What my Uncle Jim says about my grandfather, Harry Jones Smith" and write it any way you want.

First Individuals, Then Families

Although your goal should be to create family group sheets and pedigree charts, the information about each person who appears on a group sheet or pedigree chart must be known first. Therefore, to have a sense of the way the work can be organized, think of identifying genealogical events for each person who appears on your pedigree chart.

Information about one person should be gathered and recorded first, in the form of notes and documents. Then, a family group sheet and pedigree chart can be the place the facts are all put together. Family group sheets and pedigree charts represent the *presentation* of your family tree. The facts you collect before these forms are prepared represent the *research* for your family tree.

The facts gained in genealogical research are almost always oriented towards one person, with the collection of facts about that person's life. Of course, we want to link people together as married couples, as members of a family, or the blood-line connection of a person to his parents, grandparents, and so on. But, remember that all of the presentation work must be preceded by the gathering of documentation. The most important part of genealogical work, therefore, is the research to identify the significant genealogical milestones for individuals. From a collection of these facts, a family can be put together; or a pedigree chart can be extended.

Genealogical Events

The significant genealogical milestones of a person's life begin with a birth. A date and place of birth is followed by a date and place of marriage and ends with a date and place of burial. But, in-between these basic vital statistics are a myriad of events in a person's life.

We are talking about recorded events, which include anything that happened in a person's life that can be recalled from memory or from written accounts. These include, for example, a baptism, christening, or an event in which a person was recorded in history for some noteworthy deed, good or bad. The day someone entered school is a genealogical event, as is the graduation day. A name of a person mentioned in an obituary as a survivor is a genealogical event, perhaps confirming a date and place where a person lived, as well as a relationship to the deceased. In addition, an event such as a land record showing the residence for a person and the date of the land transaction is a genealogical event. Any written account of a person, however slight, is a genealogical event and adds valuable knowledge about a person's life.

All along the time-line of a person's life are events that confirm that a person lived in a particular place at a particular time. If a chronological listing of all of the events in a person's life were possible, it would give a biographical account of a person's day-by-day existence; plus it would identify all of the places a person lived. Such a complete listing is not possible unless someone has kept detailed diary entries every day for an entire lifetime. But, many of the recorded events of a person's life exist, even though they may not be obvious. For example, a record of a person's school attendance may still exist, or a record of the first piece of property a person owned exists in the form of a recorded deed in a county courthouse. A genealogist's job is to find these recorded events and extract them using the same techniques a detective uses.

Each genealogical event should have three elements: 1) a name, 2) a date, and 3) a place. For every genealogical event in a person's life, we need to identify all three elements. For a birth event, we need the person's full name, the exact date of birth, and the exact place of birth, right down to the city, county, state, and country. As we go back further in time, fewer of the recorded events exist, but even with sparse historical references, it is possible to find recorded events for people. Clearly, the more events we can identify for a person, the more we learn about them.

The discovery and collection of recorded events for a person's life is the foundation for all genealogical research. It is how we connect people from father to son, and it is how we prove that what we say is true. Just remember that what you need to know for each event is the person's name, date of event, and place of event.

Of the three elements for each genealogical event in a person's life (name, date, place) the most important one is the place. The reason for this is that the place a person lived is the same place where you will find a recorded event today. A birth record will be found residing in a state or county where the birth took place. The same is true of marriage records, death records, burial records, obituaries, land records, and virtually every other recorded event in a person's life. Therefore, special emphasis needs to be put on the place as the critical element in discovery. It comes down to this: find the place a person lived, and that's where you will find a written record of some kind. It may be in a cemetery, funeral home, museum, library, historical or genealogical society, courthouse, or in the attic of a family home. Each of these written records can be associated with a place on the ground — the jurisdiction that created the record, for example, a marriage performed in Chicago, Illinois; a deed recorded in Jasper County, Indiana; or a residence for a person confirmed in a history book written about Randolph County, North Carolina.

Basic Questions

Here are some basic questions. Answer these questions as they relate to one person, say your father. Keep in mind that you will do this same kind of Q & A for every person in your pedigree. As you answer these questions, think of other people who may help. Is there a brother or sister of your father still around? How about your own brothers or sisters? How much of the information used to answer these question came from your memory or from the memories of your relatives?

Questions about your father

1. **His name and date of birth.** What documents identify your father's full name. Who has them? Can you get copies of them? Who in your family has any kind of evidence of his birth? For the database, write down what you know about your father's name and the evidence of his birth.

2. **His place of birth.** Other than a birth certificate, what documents prove his place of birth? For example, can your aunt, your father's sister, confirm that she was at the hospital the day he was born? Was there a birth announcement in the local newspaper after his birth? Was there a baptism performed at a church? For the database, write down any facts you can recall about your father's date and place of birth.

3. **His marriage.** Do you have a copy of his marriage certificate? Was there an announcement of the marriage in a newspaper? Is there a church record of the marriage? Who performed the marriage? Can that record be obtained? Any facts regarding a person's marriage that came from your memory should be written down.

4. **His life.** What other facts about your father's life come to mind? Where was he raised? What stories do you remember about his early childhood? Where did he go to school?

5. His death. Do you have a copy of his death certificate? Was there an obituary for him in a newspaper? Where was he buried? Is there an office at the cemetery?

The answers to these questions may not all come at once. But, if you begin asking the basic questions for each person on your pedigree chart, an organization of the detective work should present itself. Now a worksheet for one person can be created in which you show the basic facts about one person, what documents you have found, and what questions need to be researched.

Filing the Notes and Documents

Using the event/place orientation for one person has another benefit. It can be used to organize your genealogical project and keep the information manageable. And, if you are using a computer to record the genealogical events, the project can be almost pleasurable. An upcoming chapter will discuss the organization of your genealogy papers — after your piles of paper begin to mount.

Your first experience with collecting notes and documents with genealogical information may not seem like much of an organization problem. You may be able to gather all of the information you have at home and from your memory and create a small notebook. But, as a warning, you should know that if you continue with this work, the paper may take over your house!

The basic questions about each person in your pedigree relate to the life of one person. But, we also find documents relating to a complete family, including parents, grandparents, children, spouses of children, and so on. In some cases, documents with genealogical data may refer to several people, several families, or several generations. Nonetheless, the collection of genealogical facts needs to be accessible for the basics of one source, one person, one event, and one place of residence.

After you have collected everything you know about yourself, including notes extracted from your memory, ID card, birth certificate, marriage certificate, notes from interviews with brothers, sisters, and parents, and so on, you will have a very neat stack of paper. Of course, you have already decided to keep these notes on standard sheets, that is, 8-1/2" x 11" notepaper. The stack of notes and documents can now be summarized. OK, so you're not a Medical Doctor, and you don't have the experience of writing down everything you discover in your examination of a patient. However, you know that your family physician has a large manila file folder with your name on it. Every time you go to the Doctor's office, he pulls out that file and adds another sheet of paper to it. You may also know that your medical file has a summary sheet on top, giving one-line descriptions of every medical fact, prescription, or diagnosis. The Doc can scan the summary sheet and get up-to-date on every treatment you have had from him over the years. (This is also where he reminds himself that your nickname is "Buffy" and you have a dog named "Blue")

An example of collecting notes relating to one person is shown below:

Summary: Albert Raymond Dollarhide

"He was born in Oakland, Douglas County, Oregon, on 19 April 1905. At the time of his birth, his family was en-route from Ft. Jones, California to a homestead near Dayton, Columbia County, Washington. He was raised on a farm a few miles south of Dayton. In 1920, the family moved to Port Angeles, Washington where Albert, by age 16, began working as a logger. He worked in logging camps between Forks and Port Angeles, Washington. More . . ."

Documentation:

Item 1 — Delayed Birth Certificate, Humboldt Co., Calif., 14 Jul 1945. Gives date of birth as 19 April 1905; place of birth as Oakland, Oregon; and names of parents as John C. and Addie (McNemar) Dollarhide. Includes affidavits from Albert's two sisters living in Eureka, California.

Item 2 — Original Birth Certificate says "baby boy Dollarhide" with date as 19 Apr 1905 but no names of parents or other information. Note by the attending physician: "These people left the county soon after the birth."

Item 3 — Driver's License, California, 1945. Gives date of birth as 19 Apr 1905 and place of birth as Oakland, Oregon, plus height, weight, color of eyes, and color of hair.

Item 4 — Interview Notes with Albert, including birth, marriage, and stories. Birth, 19 Apr 1905, Oakland, OR. Marriage, 30 Jan 1930 in Puyallup, WA to Marjory W. Wiles, dau of Elmer R. and Julia A. (Watkins) Wiles.

Item 5 — Death Certificate. Gives date of death as 18 Mar 1977 in Blaine, Whatcom Co., WA; birth, 19 Apr 1905.

Item 6 — Obituary, Seattle Times, 21 Mar 1977, date of death 18 Mar 1977. Gives date of birth 19 Apr 1905. Lived in Blaine, WA, since 1967.

Use a Notebook to Store Documents

The summary acts as a cover sheet for all of the notes and documents gathered for this one person. For all of the items listed above, the actual notes and documents were collected and stored in a notebook. One notebook can be set up for all references to people named Dollarhide and then separated in the book by the places of origin of the documents.

Thus, page numbers for the notes and documents could be identified with a place code, AL, AK, AL, etc., followed by a number such as AL1, AL2, AL3, and so on.

In the example for Albert Dollarhide, there are notes from places in California, Oregon, and Washington. These were identified with page numbers such as WA1, OR1, or CA1.

The summary sheet can also be used to refine the information into a name/date/place database.

Create a Name/Date/Place Database

The elements of name, date, and place can be extracted from every genealogical source. It is possible to create a database of event entries from all sources which would become an index to your genealogical project.

From the itemized sources listed above in the summary for Albert Dollarhide, a list of the genealogical events can be extracted into one-line entries showing a name, type of event, date of event, place of event, source, and type of record. This kind of list can be created manually, perhaps on index cards, or using a computer database program.

The suggested database will actually become an index to the events which can be reduced to three (3) types: a birth (b), a marriage (m), a death (d), or a residence (r). Add to the events the name of the person, the year of the event, the place of the event, and information about the source, or link the person to a spouse, father, or mother. Using just these basic elements, a simple database can be created as shown below. The idea is to reduce each name/date/place event to one line.

Each of the database records shown below was entered into the database in random order. But the entire list can be rearranged by name, date, place of the event, or any other order. For example, it would be possible to sort the name column and get a list of all persons named Wiles, regardless of their relationship. Another sort might list all events that took place in Ohio. Or, sort the file by the sources from one place, and so on.

As the notes and documents in a genealogy collection increase in quantity, some method of locating records quickly will be become necessary. A name/date/place database can be the solution.

Genealogical Event Index

Surname, First Name	Event | Year (b,m,d,r)	Place of Event	Source	(Rec)ord type, name of (Fa)ther, (Mo)ther, or (Sp)ouse	
Dollarhide, Albert	b1905	Oakland, OR	CA1	Rec	Delayed birth cert.
Dollarhide, Albert	r1945	Eureka, CA	CA1	Rec	Delayed birth cert.
Dollarhide, Albert	b1905	Oakland, OR	OR1	Rec	Birth certificate
Dollarhide, Albert	b1905	Oakland, OR	OR1	Fa	John C. Dollarhide
Dollarhide, Albert	b1905	Oakland, OR	OR1	Mo	Addie McNemar
Dollarhide, Albert	b1905	Oakland, OR	CA2	Rec	Driver's License
Dollarhide, Albert	r1945	Eureka, CA	CA1	Rec	Driver's License
Dollarhide, Albert	b1905	Oakland, OR	WA1	Rec	Interview notes
Dollarhide, Albert	m1930	Puyallup, WA	WA1	Sp	Marjory W. Wiles
Wiles, Marjory	m1930	Puyallup, WA	WA1	Sp	Albert Dollarhide
Wiles, Elmer R.	r1930	Seattle, WA	WA1	Sp	Julia A. Watkins
Watkins, Julia A.	r1930	Seattle, WA	WA1	Sp	Elmer R. Wiles
Dollarhide, Albert	b1905	Oakland, OR	WA2	Rec	Death certificate
Dollarhide, Albert	r1968‡	Blaine, WA	WA2	Rec	Death certificate
Dollarhide, Albert	d1977	Blaine, WA	WA2	Rec	Death certificate
Dollarhide, Albert	b1905	Oakland, OR	WA3	Rec	Obituary
Dollarhide, Albert	d1977	Blaine, WA	WA3	Rec	Obituary

Summary — Do Your Homework!

For each person on your pedigree chart, you need to do your homework. Take stock of what you know and what you can find at home that may mention a person in some way. Write down the memories you have, and build a database of genealogical events for each ancestor. Then file the notes and documents in a way that they can be stored and retrieved easily.

Every time a new name is discovered, repeat the work in this homework category. Return to your relatives with updates; and see if they can contribute more information by jogging their memories with new names, places, and dates.

Create a file or notebook for every person on your pedigree chart. As you collect the facts about one person, they can be placed in the file. Or, create a word processor text file on your computer in the same manner. After a few separate notes and documents have been gathered, the use of a summary sheet will become important. It will tell you at a glance what papers you have for each ancestor. A database of the names/dates/places from the notes and documents may become a useful method of finding records.

The next step is to gather the facts that can be gleaned from other members of your family — even your crazy relatives! And, it is also time to think of combining the facts you have gathered so far about individuals and start identifying family groups.

Step 2

Start Family Sheets

Genealogy Rule No. 5:
A relative is someone with all the information about the family you want, but died last week.

What is a Family Group Sheet?

It is time to complete a family group sheet, the basic form to record the genealogical events of a family. If you are a parent, the first family sheet should be of your family showing yourself, spouse, and children. If you are a grandparent, you may want to begin family sheets for your son or daughter, spouse, and children. In any case, creating family group sheets is a convenient way to record the details about the brothers and sisters of your parents, grandparents, great-grandparents, and so on.

A family group sheet identifies all members of a biological family with a father, mother, and all of their children listed in order of birth. The form does not include foster children, or children by a different mother or father. Therefore, for each family grouping, a separate form needs to be completed. For example, if a mother were married earlier and had children with another spouse, that family needs to be identified as another group. This may seem unfair to those who were raised in families which included step-sisters or half-brothers, but it is important to identify the members of a family by their blood relationships. What is recorded on the family group sheet is a master vital statistics arrangement. Although you are permitted to guess at dates and places, you are not permitted to lie! This is the most important record you will create in your genealogical endeavors.

Genealogy Rule No. 6:
It is a known fact that St. Peter checks all your Family Group Sheets for accuracy before you are allowed to enter the Pearly Gates.

In some cases, a family group sheet can add names of adopted children; but if this is done, it should be clearly shown on the form that these children are not the biological offspring of the father and mother shown on the form. In other words, write "adopted" next to a child's name so it is clear.

A family group sheet has space for the basic genealogical events for each person including dates and places of birth, marriage, death, and burial for each family member. For each child on the list, a name of a spouse can be given, along with a date and place of the marriage.

Note the manner of recording dates and places on the sample family group sheet on page 185. A month of a genealogical event needs to be spelled out or abbreviated — not numbered. And the year needs to be complete so it is clear. A date written as "Dec. 8th '56" is not clear, since we may be dealing with centuries, not decades in recording dates. A clear date is one that is in the military style: "8 Dec 1956." And, in recording a place, start with a smaller jurisdiction, and move to a larger one, such as, "Harrison Township, Wayne County, Indiana."

Genealogy Rule No. 7:
Treat the brothers and sisters of your ancestor as equals, even if some of them were in jail.

A family group sheet is the basic worksheet for genealogical research. While a pedigree chart identifies your direct ancestry and could be considered the culmination and presentation of your work, the family group sheet is how you get there.

The identification of each member of a family is essential to the success of your genealogical work. That means that brothers and sisters of an ancestor need to be given the same status as your ancestor. You need to identify the brothers and sisters by their full name; full birth information, including dates and places; complete marriage data, including the names of their spouses and dates of marriages; as well as death and burial information.

Seems like a lot of extra work doesn't it? But guess what. If you treat the brothers and sisters as equals, you will have many more ways to find your own ancestors. The children or later descendants of the brothers and sisters of your ancestors are your relatives — people who are sources to you for information about your own ancestor. For example, the birth certificate for my uncle gave the names of his parents, my grandparents, while the birth certificate for my father did not name his parents at all.

Involve Your Relatives

To create family group sheets, you need to enlist the help of your close relatives. A method to involve your relatives is to send them each a copy of an incomplete family group sheet on which they appear as a child or parent. Along with the form, send a sweet, folksy letter; one which reminds them that they are your favorite relatives. If you have any photographs of their family, or anything that you can share with them relating to their genealogy, send copies as examples of what a gracious and wonderful person you are. In other words, try to put them in your debt so they will respond to you. Many mothers have always known this technique well — they can elicit just about anything from their kids just by making them feel guilty.

But in making this contact, ask your relatives to add information to the family group sheets you send them and then return a copy back to you. Even if the last time you saw these people they were threatening to sic their dog on you, you need to contact them again with the news that you are now preparing the world's greatest family history and that they will be included in it.

If Your Relatives Don't Respond

Some of your relatives will try to ignore you. If they don't return a corrected family group sheet, then you may have to resort to bribery or some other devious ploy to get them to respond. For example, if you are not having success in getting your cousin Martha to return the family group sheet you sent her, try this: send Martha another group sheet, only this time indicate a bogus date of birth on the form, making her at least ten years older than she really is. Add a post-it note that says, "Did I get these dates right?" When Martha sees that incorrect date, she will have to correct it! Expect a phone call from Martha within minutes after she reads the wrong date for her birth. You could be even more devious and make Martha's date of birth two months before her parent's wedding date. Now, when Martha complains about your terrible record keeping, you can come back with, "but can you PROVE that wasn't your date of birth?" You might even get a copy of Martha's birth certificate in the mail after that one.

Visiting Relatives in Person

The best way to involve your relatives in your genealogy project is to visit them in person. See what family heirlooms they may have and what they can contribute to your knowledge of the family's history. For example, first cousins share the same grandparents. Since you are the same number of generations removed from a common ancestor, the potential exists for you to locate the same types of family records in your cousin's home as can be found in your own home. As you progress back in time, identifying more distant cousins is the technique genealogists use to add more knowledge about their own ancestors.

For each relative you can contact, go through the same homework you would do with your own immediate family members. Conduct interviews, ask about family photos, memorabilia, and so on. The only difference in doing this work with a relative is that you will do it at their home and with deference to them as the host. Ask for copies of photographs, documents, etc.; and be willing to share information and copies of materials with your relatives. Who knows, you may find that these people are actually human!

Summary — Start Family Sheets

A Family Group Sheet is the basic worksheet for genealogical research. As new information is gained, the group sheets need to be updated. Involve your relatives in creating family sheets by sending them copies they can return to you with corrected information. As new individuals are identified, family groups sheets need to be prepared as well. Return to your relatives with updated information to see if it will jog their memories and increase your knowledge further.

Step 2: Start Family Sheets

Locate More Relatives

Genealogy Rule No. 8:
Some of your cousins are lost, others are just serving time.

Become a Skip Tracer

There are more relatives to find, even if they are total strangers. At the beginning of the discovery process, we must try to locate as many relatives as possible. But if you just have a name of a person, you may need some help in finding that person. To do this, you can use the techniques of a skip tracer.

A professional skip tracer is someone who gets paid to find a person no longer living at a last known address. Skip tracers are often employed by collection agencies wanting to locate "deadbeat" customers who have skipped out of paying their bills. Skip tracers are also used to locate missing persons for a variety of reasons, such as finding a person who is an heir to an estate. Lawyers use skip tracers to locate potential witnesses, or to contact persons regarding pending court cases. And private individuals often use skip tracers to locate missing children or adoptive children and parents.

A missing person may not want to be found. There are persons who change their names, change their residence, and go out of their way to be "lost" for whatever reason. In such cases, even skip tracers have a problem locating them — because outside of official government investigations, inquiries into the lives of private individuals are often restricted and difficult to accomplish.

Check the Death Index

Before looking for a relative's address, confirm that the person is still alive. The best way is to check the Social Security Master Death Index which is available from several different sources. Even without knowing a person's social security number, it is still possible to determine if the person is in the death index. One of the easiest of these look-up services is found on the Internet at www.myfamily.com where a search in the Social Security Master Death Index can be made by the surname or optional first name or defined by a particular place in the U.S. where a person died.

About 95 percent of the persons who died between 1962 and 1999 can be found in the death index. If a person is listed in the death index, you will learn the deceased person's social security number and the last residence for a person. With the name and social security number, you can obtain a copy of the deceased's application for a social security account which was filled in by the person and gives his/her full name, date and place of birth, place of residence, name of parents, occupation, and name of employer. The myfamily.com site provides a free service and will prepare a written letter addressed to the Social Security Administration which you can print and mail, requesting a copy of any deceased person's application for a social security card.

What Do You Know?

Assuming your lost relative is still alive, and before starting the search, ask yourself and others in the family what you know about the missing person you want to find. Where did he/she last live? Was the person married? Did he have children? Did you have mutual friends? Were they in school with you? What kind of job did the person have? Where did he go on vacations? What church did he attend? Did he have a family doctor? If so, is that Doctor still in practice? Was your subject in the military? Was the person a member of a club? Now prepare a list of known facts about the person. List everything you know. The last place lived is the starting point; but if you know any places where the person lived, try to create a chronological list of places where a search may be done.

Tricks of the Trade

A professional skip tracer will often stretch the limits of moral and legal considerations, passing himself off as someone else to obtain information. Skip tracer Eugene Ferraro, the author of the book, *You Can Find Anyone: A Complete Guide on How to Locate Missing Persons* (Santa Ana, CA: Marathon Press, 1989), starts off on the first page with the statement, "Some of the methods and procedures presented in this text may be illegal in your state." The techniques suggested by Ferraro include misrepresenting yourself when contacting schools, former employers, or former landlords in locating a missing person.

The tricks of the trade of a skip tracer include such things as phone calls to an apartment owner where the missing person once lived, saying you are also an apartment owner and have been left with some valuable item that needs to be returned to the missing party... "Could you please give the party's forwarding address?" Or when calling a party who may be reluctant to give out information, Ferraro says to look up a florist shop near where the person lives, call the party, and say you are from that flower shop and have a paid floral arrangement to deliver but need the address of the person.

Most missing persons are not lost — they are living and working somewhere at an address where a letter could be sent; they have a telephone; their names have not changed; and they do not think of themselves as "missing" at all. Genealogists who want to find missing relatives can apply the research techniques a professional skip tracer would use to locate them and save paying fees that could be as high as $300 per day by doing the research themselves.

However, genealogists looking for a lost relative may find that many of the techniques employed by skip tracers only apply to persons who have just recently moved — and may not apply to a person whose last known address was in 1925, for example. But, a genealogist may find these methods helpful, particularly in locating the residence of a person who is still living or recently died.

To locate a living person, it is a matter of starting with what you know about the person and attempt to find the last known address. You may have some information that will reveal clues about where to look next, or there may be other members of your family who can add to what you know about the missing relative.

Telephone Directory Search

Telephone directories are an easy way to locate a person in the U.S. but only if you have access to them all. At one time, larger libraries usually had an excellent collection of current phone directories covering much of the country. But more recently, with the break-up of AT&T into regional phone companies, the libraries no longer receive the directories for free. As a result, the library collection may not be current or as complete anymore. In any case, the library is still a good starting point for locating phone books outside of your area.

Some larger libraries have purchased the current telephone directory listings in the form of microfiche which are very complete and up-to-date. And, some libraries have the same version available on CD-ROM. To find out what your local library has to offer in the way of telephone books, give them a call — telephone books are usually located in the "Reference" section of a library.

Search for Names on the Internet

There are several sites on the Internet where free telephone directory searches are possible. A convenient site is at www.myfamily.com where one can type a name and get a list of all persons with that name taken from phone books across the country, including an address and a phone number. Another is the "White Pages" option of the Microsoft Home Page at www.msn.com. A search at these sites can be specific to a last name and optional first name for person, plus it can be specific to a certain place. Search options may also include a "reverse search," where it is possible to look for a current resident's name when all that is known is an address — a useful search for learning the name of a person living in a house once occupied by a relative who has moved. (The current resident of a house may know where the former resident moved,)

Genealogy Rule #9:
Genealogists with computers and the Internet think they don't have to leave home to do their research anymore — and they may be right!

Special searches for any person are available for a fee at www.1800ussearch.com using public records such as driver's licenses, vehicle registrations, and court records from some states. They state that "it is possible to obtain addresses and phone numbers of neighbors of a person, plus names of the subject's children, spouses, other people at the same address, additional phone numbers, and a history of a person's current and previous addresses for the past ten years. It may also be possible to obtain a summary of a person's assets, professional licenses, property ownership and value, lien filings, civil judgements, and any bankruptcies."

Another people-finding service on the Internet for a fee is at www.searchco.com which states "All we need is the name of the person you are searching for, and we will search the national public information databases totaling over 600 million names. Our database search is extensive and thorough. Our sources include (but are not limited to): National consumer credit bureau files, national change of address, voters registration, census data, state drivers license (where available), social security records, death index, publishers mailing lists, and other public records. We do more than just phone books. You will receive a report including names, addresses, and phone numbers of the most likely matches. It is up to you to make contact with the people on the list. We can't guarantee you'll find your person, but most people have a 'paper trail,' and our databases provide a very high success rate."

City Directories

Virtually every city in America has a city directory published every year, except for the very largest cities. (New York City's last city directory listing every household was in 1932). The R. L. Polk Company is the largest publisher of city directories; and for the larger cities in the U.S., this company maintains regional offices. Directories published for the cities in Western Washington, or about 150 miles from Seattle, Washington, for example, can all be seen in their office in downtown Seattle; and they allow the public to browse through the current directories in person. To locate an R. L. Polk office near you, check your local phone book.

In addition, state libraries, usually located at a state capital, are good sources for city directories within a particular state. But the repository for city directories with the best collection for a particular community is the public library in the city itself. A search of directories for a particular city may span over 100 years of published city directories.

City directories give more information than phone books. In addition to a person's name, the occupation of the person is given, which can prove to be another clue to locating information about a person from a past employer. Often, the name of a woman will be listed if she is the head of a house; and if widowed, the name of her husband may be indicated. By searching multiple years, it may be possible to determine in which year her husband died. In some city directories, even names and ages of children are given.

It may be possible to obtain copies from a city directory for the page containing a particular surname by writing to a library stating your request for a particular time period. Addresses and phone numbers for all American libraries are listed in Bowker's *American Library Directory*, a two-volume publication found at virtually all libraries across the country.

The Library of Congress in Washington, DC, has the largest collection of city directories for towns, cities, and county-wide directories, some dating back to the 18ᵗʰ Century. The method of finding out if the Library of Congress has a directory for a particular year and city is to request photocopies from the city directory — and if they don't have the one you request, you'll be informed. If they do have it, you will have saved a step in the process; and they will inform you of the cost to make photocopies. For example, say you are looking for William Winkerhaven in Buffalo, New York, for about 1952. Write and ask for photocopies from the 1951-3 city directories for Buffalo for all pages containing the surname Winkerhaven. Write to: Library of Congress, Photo-duplication Services, Washington, DC 20540.

Friends and Neighbors

If you have an address for a subject, find out who were the neighbors of the person by using phone books and city directories. The R.L. Polk directories include a cross-street index listing streets and avenues, sometimes called a "reverse index." With a given address, these directories can be used to locate the neighbors of your subject easily. If any of the neighbors are still living there — which can be confirmed by comparing an earlier city directory with the current one — they are sources of information about your subject, and a letter to them asking about your relative's whereabouts may pay off. Old friends and neighbors have a tendency to stay in touch by way of annual Christmas cards; and if so, the address of your lost relative may be in the hands of one of his or her former neighbors.

One method of writing to a total stranger who may have been a neighbor of your lost relative is to write a letter to the lost relative, then enclose that letter with a letter addressed to the person who was a neighbor. Ask the neighbor to forward the enclosed letter to your lost relative . . . if they know the address. This relieves the neighbor from giving out the address to you, but allows them to send the letter along. Include a stamped envelope to make it easy for the neighbor to forward the letter.

Genealogy Rule #10:
If your lost relative owes money to someone, that person will always be willing to help you find him.

Employers

The R. L. Polk directories may give the occupation of your subject and often the name of an employer. If so, you now have another potential source to contact. Neighbors may remember where a person worked as well, and your memories and those of other family members may reveal the name of an employer.

Skip tracers often employ a pretext — they call it a "gag" or a "pitch" — to contact an employer. For example, skip tracers write a letter stating they are of the "XYZ Company" and wish to confirm employment for the subject. They say they are conducting a "pre-employment" investigation on the subject and ask for verification of employment, duties, and other vitals, such as date of birth, marriage, children, and educational background. As a genealogist, however, your approach may be a humanitarian request for information about the subject, stressing that you are trying to reunite family members.

Schools

If you know that your subject attended a particular school or college, a phone call may be useful. Use Directory Assistance to obtain a phone number for the school and ask for the Student Records section. Public school administrators have become very protective of their current records, even for prospective employers who are verifying diplomas or degrees earned by a person. But, for genealogists looking for a person who attended a school years ago, the requests can be made on a personal level. Making a request over the phone may allow you to learn if the person attended the school, of his vital statistics, or perhaps a forwarding address where the records were sent when the student left the school. In addition, the most complete set of school annuals will be found in that same school's library; and this is a place to confirm a year when a person attended a school. It will also provide names of people who were in school with your subject, people who may be easier to locate than your subject and can be contacted today.

If the school administration refuses to provide any information about a former student, ask about any school alumni or reunion committees for the school. The school administrator should not object to giving out this information, and you should learn the name of a person in charge of alumni or reunions for a particular school year or number of years. These groups are very good at locating former students, and there is generally a person in charge of keeping a mailing list of former graduates. As an example, I graduated from West Seattle High School in 1960. In 1970, 1980, 1990, and 2000, I received a letter from the high school reunion committee inviting me to a high school reunion, even though I was at a different address for each of those reunion years. I fully expect to get another announcement for a reunion in the year 2010.

Nursing Home Records

Nursing homes maintain files on their patients; and if you know that your subject was ever in a nursing home, you can try calling or writing for information. Medical records are not obtainable by unauthorized persons; but as a genealogist, your request should be for purposes of locating a family member. Depending on the nursing facility, an appeal may be successful in obtaining information from the face sheet of the patient's file (which gives vital statistics, social security number, address, nearest kin, and so on). If all you can obtain is the name of the nearest kin of the subject, you will have accomplished something worthwhile.

Newspaper Ads

If your subject lived in a smaller town or rural area, you may have good results by placing a classified ad in the "personals" section of the local newspaper. I once placed a $12.00 classified ad in the *Albany Ledger*, a weekly newspaper of Albany, Missouri, which read, "Seattle attorney looking for heirs of Lafayette Black, a resident of Gentry County, Missouri, from about 1880 to 1920. His known children were Grant, Elizabeth, and William Black. All responses will be held private and confidential." The newspaper staff must have decided that the ad was unique because they placed it on the front page. I received 12 letters, which resulted in identifying over 50 living descendants of Lafayette Black.

To find the name and address of a newspaper near where your subject lived, use the *Gale Directory of Publications and Broadcast Media* (published by Gale Research, Detroit) in your local library. It lists all newspapers in the United States and Canada, along with current advertising rates, and everything else needed to place a classified advertisement in a particular newspaper.

Deeds and Voter Registrations

If a person lived in one county for a number of years and owned property, it is certain that you will find your subject's name in the county deed indexes.

For locating your lost relative, a starting point might be to check that county's grantee-grantor index for the time period when you know the subject was in a particular county. A recorded deed will give an address for both the grantor (seller) and grantee (buyer) of real property. In years before about 1920, the address may have been part of a beginning statement such as "John Brown of Johnson, County." In later years, the deed will include a complete street address, city and state (and zip-code after about 1962). Indexed along with deeds are records of exchanges and actions dealing with real property such as liens, easements, power-of-attorney exchanges, or judgements. They are all indexed by both the seller's and buyer's names; and anyone can see them because deed indexes are public records.

As an example of using deeds to locate someone, say your subject owned property in the county but moved away about October 1985. If the deed were recorded after he left the property in question — say the property sale did not close until January 1986 — the seller's *new address* would be shown on the recorded deed.

The best way to conduct deed research is to do it in person or have a person living in that county do it for you. You can write to a county office where recorded deeds are kept asking for a check of the grantee/grantor index. There are three excellent books genealogists can use to determine who is the keeper of the various court records for every county in the U.S. along with an address of where to write:

- *Ancestry's Red Book: American State, County and Town Sources,* Alice Eichholz, Editor, (Orem, UT: Ancestry, Inc., rev. 1992, 864 pp, $49.95). The *Red Book* is very thorough, showing all 3,146 counties in the U.S., but also identifies all 1,557 New England towns along with an address for each and can be used for writing for vital and court records. This book has the best set of maps showing the location of all counties and towns for each state.

- *The Handy Book for Genealogists,* (Logan, UT: Everton Publishers, 9th edition, 1999, 600 pp, $34.95). The county information is condensed into easy-to-follow listings for each state, along with maps showing the location of the counties for each state. The *Handy Book* does not include New England towns but is easier to use than the *Red Book* for finding the counties of the U.S.

- **The County Courthouse Book,** Elizabeth Petty Bentley, compiler, (Baltimore: Genealogical Publishing Co., Inc., 2nd edition, 1995, 395 pp, $34.95). Based on surveys mailed to each of the 3,141 counties in the U.S. and the 1,557 New England towns, the data from the county and town officials who returned the surveys (about 65%) is very valuable and more comprehensive than either the *Red Book* or *Handy Book*. On the other hand, there are no maps in the *County Courthouse Book*.

Also kept at the county level, **Voter Registrations** are current lists of registered voters for a county; and anyone can ask to look at them because they are public records. Older lists may still be maintained by the county officer in charge, but are not readily available, so a letter asking if the voter lists for a certain number of years are accessible would be in order. Copies of the voter's application may also be available which has vital statistics about a person. Older lists are generally maintained in a storage room somewhere in the courthouse.

To access these records, it is best to do it in person. But, by contacting a person in the county of question, someone can visit the courthouse for you. The best way to locate a person in a county who can visit a courthouse for you is to contact a local genealogical society. A good list of American genealogical societies is in Elizabeth Petty Bentley, editor, *The Genealogist's Address Book* (Baltimore: Genealogical Publishing Co., Inc., 3rd edition, 1998).

Military Records

If your lost relative was ever in the military, there may be a way to locate the person by using a locator service operated by one of the military branches. The Army, Navy, and Air Force all have locator services, designed to find a veteran's current address from official sources. The National Archives and Records Administration, National Personnel Records Center (Military Records Facility) is located at 9700 Page Ave., St. Louis, MO 63132-5100. Write for a form SF-80 to request copies from any soldier or sailor's military file.

Summary — Locate More Relatives

Contact with your relations can be an important part of genealogical research since your relatives share ancestors with you. Relatives are a source of information and may enhance your knowledge of your ancestry.

To locate lost relatives, some special techniques can be employed using the tricks of the skip tracer's trade. Telephone directory searches, Internet searches, city directories, friends and neighbors, employers, schools, military, and other resources may provide information about lost relatives.

Get the Vital Records

Get a Death Certificate

For every person on your pedigree chart and for every brother or sister of an ancestor, you need to obtain a death certificate (assuming they are dead). If there were five brothers and sisters in an ancestor's family, a death certificate for each sibling will give five different sources about the same parents including places where the family lived; names of spouses; names of cemeteries; names of funeral directors and perhaps other facts about a family. For example, if a death certificate for your ancestor failed to provide the name of the deceased's mother, a sibling's death certificate may give the full maiden name. Again, the rule is to treat the brothers and sisters of your ancestors as equals. That means you need to obtain death certificates for all of them.

So, to get started, it is time to write for copies of death certificates for your parents, grandparents, and close relatives who have died. If you know the state in which a person died, a copy of a death certificate is easy to obtain. Statewide registration of vital records started during the period 1900-1920, and all but a few states have vital records from about 1910 forward. It is a matter of writing to the state vital statistics office and requesting a copy a death certificate.

Genealogy Rule #11:
Death certificates are rarely filled in by the person who died.

The standard death certificate form for all states includes important information about the deceased. In addition to the cause and circumstances surrounding the death, the certificate includes the name of the person's father and maiden name of the person's mother. The exact date and place of birth and death should also be on the certificate. Further, you may learn the name of the person's spouse, the name of a funeral director, the name of the cemetery where the body was interred, and the name of the "informant" (the person who provided the information for the death certificate). On more recent death certificates, you will learn the deceased's social security number. The names, dates, and places you will find on a death certificate will almost always lead you to further records.

It is estimated that at least 20 percent of all death certificates have a mistake on them. The most common mistake is the spelling of the name of the person; but mistakes in dates, places, and names of parents are also common. Since the one piece of information you can count on is the place and date the person died, you need the death certificate to get the other evidence relating to a person's death. Putting these other items of evidence together is how you prove something. One document, one memory, or just one source is not enough.

Get More Vital Records

With a death certificate in hand for your ancestors and their siblings, you now have more records to get. For each death record, you need to follow up any clues you learn which may lead you to even more records concerning a person's death. But, you say, "I already know his date and place of death, why do I need all these other death records?" Well, every document you obtain is building a case. One document is not enough, because the document may be in error. One memory is not enough because it may be repeating an error passed down from generation to generation. And, one source is not enough because, to prove something, you need more than one source. Therefore, before you can prove anything, you need to build a case by obtaining every document that is available relating to a genealogical event. That means you have many more things to do after getting a death certificate for someone. But, if you do the extra work and get the other documents, you will learn something new on virtually every new document you get. For example, a death certificate may mention the name of the funeral director, the cemetery where the body was interred, and perhaps the name of a relative as the informant. Each of these pieces of information will open the door to even more information about the person.

Get a Funeral Record

A death certificate may mention the name and location of a funeral director. Contact the funeral home and ask if there are records concerning the person's death and funeral service. A funeral record may include names of survivors and names of the persons responsible for the funeral expenses in addition to biographical information about the deceased. Modern funeral records are full of genealogical information about the person who died and may include copies of newspaper obituaries, death certificates, printed eulogies, funeral programs, and other details about the person. A reference to a burial, cremation, or cemetery should be found here as well.

Genealogy Rule #12:
When visiting a funeral home, wear old clothes, no make-up, and look like you have about a week to live — the funeral director will give you anything you ask for if he thinks you may be a customer soon.

Generally, funeral directors are very easy to talk to and they are usually cooperative (they want your family's business). To get an address for a funeral home anywhere in the U.S. or Canada, call or visit any funeral director in your area and ask if you can use is directory of funeral homes, *The Yellow Book*. This annual directory gives the name, address, and phone number of every funeral home in North America. *The Yellow Book's* database of American and Canadian funeral homes can also be found on the Internet at www.funeralnet.com.

Even if the old name of a funeral home is not listed in a current directory, it should be possible to locate the current funeral home holding the records of an earlier one. These businesses rarely go out of business, but are more often taken over by another funeral director. If at one time a town had two or three funeral homes, but only one today, the *Yellow Book* is still the source for finding the current funeral home in that town, which can lead you to information about the older funeral home. The current funeral directors are very well versed in the history of funeral homes in their area, including those that may have changed their names since a death certificate was issued. They are also experts on the location of cemeteries in their area. If you write to a funeral director, include a self-addressed stamped envelope (SASE) as a courtesy, and to make it easy for him to return something to you.

Get a Cemetery Record

If the name of a cemetery is mentioned on the death certificate, a cemetery is now a potential source of information about the person who died. There may be a record in the office of the cemetery, and the gravestone inscription may be revealing as well. When you contact a funeral home, ask about the cemetery where the person was buried, and whether they have an address or phone number for the cemetery office, or at least know who might be the keeper of records for the cemetery. At the same time, ask the funeral director for the names of monument sellers and stone masons who cater to cemeteries in the area. As a backup, a local stone mason may have a record of a monument inscription for the deceased's gravestone.

Genealogy Rule #13:
The cemetery where your ancestor was buried does not have perpetual care, has no office, is accessible only by a muddy road, and has snakes, tall grass, and lots of bugs . . . and many of the old gravestones are in broken pieces, stacked in a corner under a pile of dirt.

To locate a cemetery anywhere in the United States, a special list can be obtained from the Internet site for the United States Geological Survey (USGS) within their Geographic Names Information System (GNIS). The GNIS contains the names of nearly two million place-names (map features) in America, of which about 107,000 are cemeteries. As an example, the name of a particular feature can be found by asking for a name, such as "Dollarhide," and feature type, such as "Cemetery," the following list would appear:

Geographic Names Information System Query Results

Dollarhide — Cemetery
    Three Feature records have been selected from GNIS :

    Dollarhide Cemetery
        Feature Type: cemetery

State: Arkansas
County: Little River
USGS 7.5' x 7.5' Map: Foreman
Latitude: 334740N
Longitude: 0942440W

Dollarhide Cemetery
Feature Type: cemetery
State: Ohio
County: Highland
USGS 7.5' x 7.5' Map: Greenfield
Latitude: 391915N
Longitude: 0832821W

Dollarhide Cemetery
Feature Type: cemetery
State: Virginia
County: Wise
USGS 7.5' x 7.5' Map: Coeburn
Latitude: 365658N
Longitude: 0822437W

With the query results above, a map can be produced and printed for each feature site selected. The Internet address to query the database of the GNIS is as follows:
http://mapping.usgs.gov/www/gnis/gnisform.html

Get an Obituary

A newspaper obituary was probably published soon after the person's death. Old newspapers from the town where the person died are usually available in the local public library. They may be on microfilm. Go to your own library and ask for the **American Library Directory**, published by R.R. Bowker, Inc., of New York. Every library in the U.S. has this book. Get the address for the library nearest the place your subject died, and write a letter requesting a copy of that person's obituary from the local newspaper.

If the library responds but says it is unable to look for an obituary or make copies for you, then you may need to find a person living in that town to go to the library for you. Your best way to locate such a person is to write to a local genealogical society and ask if they know someone who can do a bit of research for you. Most genealogical societies have a volunteer who responds to such requests, and there will most likely be a small fee for this service. A good list of American genealogical societies is in Elizabeth Petty Bentley, editor, **The Genealogist's Address Book** (Baltimore: Genealogical Publishing Co., Inc., 3rd edition, 1998).

Your local library should also have a copy of the two-volume publication, **Newspapers on Microform**, a listing of newspapers for all states and cities in the U.S. which have been microfilmed, it tells what repository holds the microfilm. This publication can be used to identify and order rolls of microfilm for use at your local library through the national Interlibrary Loan program.

Get a Social Security record

If a person died within the last 35 years or so, the death certificate probably includes the deceased's social security number. If so, you are in luck. You can write for a copy of the deceased's original application for a social security card, a Form SS-5. Birth and death records are primary sources, but they were prepared by someone other the person himself. On the other hand, an application for a social security account is a primary source prepared by the person himself. Since 1935, virtually every working person in America has applied for a social security account. In doing so, the applicant wrote his full name, date of birth, place of birth, name of father, maiden name of mother, place of residence, place and name of employer, and a signature.

There is no better genealogical source than this record — and a copy of the application form can be obtained from the Social Security Administration, even for a person who is suspected of being an ancestor and you have no proof — as long as the person is dead, that is.

There is an index to the Social Security file called the Social Security Master Death Index. It needs to be consulted to see if the person is listed. Even without knowing a person's social security number, it is still possible to determine if the person is in the death index. One of the easiest of the lookup services is found on the Internet at www.myfamily.com where a search in the Social Security Master Death Index can be made by the surname or optional first name, or defined by a particular place in the U.S. where a person died. About 95 percent of the persons who died between 1962 and 2000 can be found in this death index. If a person is listed in the death index, you will learn the deceased person's social security number, and the last residence for a person. With the name and social security number you can obtain a copy of the deceased's application for a social security account. The myfamily.com Internet site provides a free service to prepare a written letter addressed to the Social Security Administration which you can print and mail, requesting a copy of any deceased person's application for a social security card.

Genealogy Rule #14:
A Social Security record is better than a birth certificate because few people had anything to do with the information on their own birth certificate.

Get Other Possible Death Records

Other records may be available if you know a name, date, and place of death for a person. Here are some possibilities:

Probate Records pertaining to the deceased's estate may be located in a county courthouse and may provide important information about the heirs of the deceased. Probate records may include dockets (court calendars), recorded wills, administrator's records, inventories of estates, sheriff's sales, and judgements.

Insurance Papers. If the deceased had insurance, there is undoubtably a record of the death within the insurance company's files. These give much more information concerning the deceased's survivors and the disposition of an estate.

Coroner and Medical Examiner Records exist for any person who died under suspicious conditions; for whom an autopsy was performed; or, in most cases, for people who died outside of a hospital. Coroner records are public records kept at the county level in virtually all states.

Military Records for deceased veterans are public records. The National Archives and Records Administration, National Personnel Records Center (Military Records Facility) is located at 9700 Page Ave., St. Louis, MO 63132-5100. Write for a form SF-80 to request copies from any soldier or sailor's military file.

Church Records. A death record may be recorded within a church's records. These records may also give information about a burial.

Get a Birth Record

If the death certificate gives a date and place of birth, you can write for a copy of a birth certificate from a state vital statistics office. If the date of birth predates statewide registration (about 1900-1920), a birth record may still be available from a county courthouse near the place the person was born. Typically, a birth certificate will confirm a person's date and place of birth and names of parents. In later records, the name of the attending physician and hospital will be given. However, of all of the vital records, birth records are the most restrictive. Generally, a birth certificate will not be issued unless the request is from the person or parents named on the certificate, or from a legal representative. Most states have a period of restriction before a birth certificate will be issued to anyone, and the period can range from 25 to 100 years. If a death certificate or other proof of death can be produced, then a birth certificate for the same person will be much easier to obtain.

Sources for a Person's Birth

The following list identifies some sources which may provide a person's date of and place of birth. In some cases, the source may only give a person's name and age from which an approximate date of birth can be determined:

- ☐ Application for employment
- ☐ Baby's dedication record
- ☐ Baby picture
- ☐ Baptismal record
- ☐ Biography in a book
- ☐ Birth certificate
- ☐ Birth announcement
- ☐ Burial permit
- ☐ Business license application
- ☐ Cemetery sextons' record
- ☐ Census indexes
- ☐ Census population schedules
- ☐ Census mortality schedules
- ☐ Census soundex indexes
- ☐ Christening records
- ☐ Church confirmation records
- ☐ Church membership records
- ☐ Church burial records
- ☐ City directories
- ☐ Company employment
- ☐ Coroner/Medical Examiner's record
- ☐ Correspondence
- ☐ Cremation records
- ☐ Death certificate
- ☐ Deed records
- ☐ Doctors' birth record
- ☐ Doctors' patient record
- ☐ Draft registration records
- ☐ Drivers' license
- ☐ Driving history records
- ☐ Family Bible
- ☐ Family papers
- ☐ Family tree needlepoint
- ☐ Fraternal/club records
- ☐ Funeral home records
- ☐ History books
- ☐ Homestead records
- ☐ Hospital patient records
- ☐ Immigration records
- ☐ Insurance ID card
- ☐ Insurance company records
- ☐ Lineage society application
- ☐ Marriage license
- ☐ Military burial records
- ☐ Military personnel record
- ☐ Mortgage records
- ☐ Military medical records
- ☐ Newspaper gossip columns
- ☐ Non-population censuses
- ☐ Nursing Home records
- ☐ Obituary
- ☐ Passport application
- ☐ Pension records
- ☐ Permit to transport a body out of state
- ☐ Petition for land grants
- ☐ Probate records
- ☐ Professional license
- ☐ Resume
- ☐ School annual
- ☐ School attendance records
- ☐ School credentials record
- ☐ Ship passenger lists
- ☐ Social Security work history
- ☐ Social Security Account Application
- ☐ Social Security Master Death Index
- ☐ Stone masons' records
- ☐ Title insurance records
- ☐ Tombstone inscriptions
- ☐ Union card
- ☐ Union dues record
- ☐ Vital Statistics Indexes
- ☐ Voter registration

Get a Marriage Record

Marriage records offer one the most complete set of documents that can be used by genealogists. From the early days of European history, a recorded marriage was required to legitimatize any heirs resulting from that marriage. Marriages were first recorded within church records, confirming a legal union of two people; and the records were carefully preserved because of the legal implications. As a result, if two people were married in a church, there is an excellent chance of finding a written reference to that marriage, even for many of the marriages that occurred more than 500 years ago.

Since the beginnings of the American colonies, most marriages were recorded, whether in a parish church, town hall, or a county courthouse. Of all written manuscript records, American marriage records are more complete and go back farther in time than any other.

For the last two centuries, virtually all marriage records were civil records first recorded in a town hall or county courthouse. For over half of the states, marriages are still kept at the county level. From about 1950-1975, statewide registration of marriages began for several of the states; and today are found in the same vital statistics office that maintains birth, death, or divorce records. In addition, there may be a record of the marriage in a church where the marriage took place. In most of the U.S. states, you need to know the county where the marriage took place; and in the New England states and New York, you need to know the town where the marriage took place.

Where to find Official Birth, Death, Marriage, and Divorce Records

About every three or four years, the Government Printing Office (GPO) prints and distributes a little booklet, **Where to Write for Birth, Death, and Marriage Records,** published for the National Center for Health Statistics (NCHS). The GPO booklet is usually out-of-date the same week it is released.

Genealogy Rule #15:
The application for a death certificate you want insists that you provide the maiden name of the deceased's mother — which is exactly what you don't know and is the reason you are trying to get the death certificate in the first place.

Genealogists have several other sources for this information including the Social Security Administration's general information 800 number (Check your white pages. The number is different in different regions of the country.) which is a place to find out where the state vital statistics offices are for each state and U.S. territory, along with the fee for certified copies of birth and death records.

You need information about where to get birth, death, or other vital records. You have a computer with a connection to the Internet. So, why not use your keyboard fingers to do the walking? There are some really great web-sites on the Internet where you can locate the vital statistics offices for all states and obtain up-to-date information about each office's policies, fees, and more.

National Center for Health Statistics

The same GPO booklet mentioned earlier is now available on the Internet, and hopefully, the information will be updated more often. The NCHS Internet website for "How to obtain birth, death, marriage, and divorce certificates" is located at:
http://www.cdc.gov

The VitaCheck Network

This service has an Internet, voice, and fax network setup to help people get a certified copy of a birth certificate, death certificate, marriage certificate and other vital records. VitaChek provides the information on how to obtain a vital record from their listings of participating state agencies. Their Home Page is located at http://www.vitalcheck.com, where you can click on a U.S. map for a particular state, or get a phone list, a fax list, or a mailing list for all vital statistics offices. Most of the statewide vital statistics offices participate with the VitaCheck network — in fact several of the states refer users to the VitaCheck service exclusively for on-line ordering of records. VitalCheck provides for phone, mail, fax, or on-line ordering of certified copies of vital records, using your Visa, MasterCard, Discover, or American Express card.

However, the VitalCheck service adds at least a $5.00 fee to the fee you would already pay to a vital statistics office to obtain copies of vital records. They do add shipping costs.

Vital Records Information Service

This is a free Internet service which is very complete. It includes web pages for the U.S. and each of the fifty states, and American Samoa, Canal Zone, District of Columbia, Guam, Northern Mariana Islands, Puerto Rico, and the Virgin Islands. In addition, it links to another web page for foreign vital records web sites with information about vital statistics from Canada, England, Ireland, Australia, New Zealand, Hungary, Poland, and Slovakia.

Access the Vital Records Information service http://vitalrec.com/, where a list of states and territories will be presented. Click on the state of interest, and you will be taken to that state web page. As an example, the Alabama web page indicates that birth and death records are available since January 1908; and the fee for a certified copy is $12.00. In Alabama, copies can be obtained by anyone for birth records more than 125 years old and death records more than 25 years old; otherwise you must be immediate family or have written permission from the next of kin.

Also, at the Alabama page, you would learn that vital records are available from the state vital statistics office in Montgomery and through a statewide computer system that became fully operational in 67 counties in June 1996. Within the state, authorized applicants can walk into any county health department and get any Alabama vital record, regardless of where the event took place in the state. The wait is usually no more than 20 to 30 minutes.

In addition, the Vital Records Information page for Alabama has a link to the addresses of all Alabama county vital statistics registrars. And, the reader is directed to the Department of Archives and History in Montgomery for early county birth and death records. You can access the Alabama page directly by using the web address, http://vitalrec.com/al.html and any other state by replacing "al" with the two-letter code for the state you want.

Genealogy Rule #16:
When you contact the state vital statistics office in your home state and ask if they are "on-line," and they respond, "on-what?," you may have a problem.

State Vital Records Offices on the Internet

Thirty-seven of the fifty states have their vital record's information available on-line (at this writing). In addition to the policies, fees, and addresses, most have the means of downloading an application form as an Adobe Acrobat file which can be printed directly to your printer. For states which do not provide vital statistics information on-line, see the VitaCheck or Vital Records Information above. The names of the state offices with their Internet addresses are shown below:

Alaska
Bureau of Vital Statistics
http://www.hss.state.ak.us/dph/bvs/bvs_home.htm

Arkansas
Department of Health
http://www.healthyarkansas.com/certificates/certificates.html#Vital

California
Office of Vital Records
http://www.dhs.cahwnet.gov/hisp/chs/OVR/Ordercert.htm

Colorado
Vital Records Office
www.quickinfo.net/madi/comadi.html
This site includes an index to Colorado marriages and divorces from 1975 which can be searched on-line.

Connecticut
Health Dept.-Vital Records
http://www.state.ct.us/dph/OPPE/hpvital.htm

Hawaii
State Department of Health
http://www.state.hi.us/health/records/vr_howto.html

Illinois
Division of Vital Records
www.idph.state.il.us/vital/vitalhome.htm

Indiana
Vital Records Department
www.state.in.us/isdh/bdcertifs/bdcert.html

Iowa
Department of Public Health
www.idph.state.ia.us/pa/vr.htm

Kansas
Office of Vital Statistics
www.kdhe.state.ks.us/vital/index.html

Kentucky
Office of Vital Statistics
http://ukcc.uky.edu/~vitalrec/
This site has an on-line **Vital Records Index** which includes Kentucky deaths, 1911-1992; marriages, 1973-1993; and divorces, 1973-1993.

Louisiana
Vital Records Registry
www.dhh.state.la.us/oph/vrinfo.htm

Maryland
Division of Vital Records
www.sos.state.md.us/sos/html/vitalrec.html

Massachusetts
Bureau of Health Statistics
www.magnet.state.ma.us/dph/vitrecs.htm

Michigan
Division for Vital Records and Health Statistics
www.mdch.state.mi.us/pha/osr/vitalrec.htm

Minnesota
Department of Health, Birth and Death Records
www.health.state.mn.us/forms.html

Mississippi
Vital Records
www.msdh.state.ms.us/phs/forms/form522i.htm

Missouri
Bureau of Vital Records
http://www.health.state.mo.us/BirthAndDeathRecords/BirthAndDeathRecords.html

Montana
Vital Records
www.imt.net/~corkykn/vital.html

Nebraska
Vital Statistics
www.hhs.state.ne.us/ced/bicert.htm

New Jersey
Bureau of Vital Statistics
www.state.nj.us/health/vital/vs11.htm

New York
Vital Records Section
www.health.state.ny.us/nysdoh/consumer/vr/geninst.htm

North Carolina
Vital Records
http://www.schs.state.nc.us/SCHS/certificates/

North Dakota
Division of Vital Records:
www.health.state.nd.us/ndhd/admin/vital/index.htm

Ohio
State Vital Statistics Unit
http://www.odh.state.oh.us/Birth/vitalrec.htm
Visit the Ohio Historical Society's web site which has an **Ohio Death Certificate Index** for the period 1913-1937, located at
http://dbs.ohiohistory.org/dindex/search.cfm

Oklahoma
Vital Records Service
www.health.state.ok.us/program/vital/brec.html

Oregon
Vital Records
http://www.ohd.hr.state.or.us/chs/certif/certfaqs.htm

Pennsylvania
State Department of Health, Vital Records
www.health.state.pa.us/hpa/apply_bd.htm

South Dakota
Department of Health, Vital Records
www.state.sd.us/doh/vitalrec/vital.htm

Texas
Department of Health, Bureau of Vital Statistics
www.tdh.state.tx.us/bvs/default.htm

Utah
Bureau of Vital Records
http://hlunix.hl.state.ut.us/bvr/html/certificates.html

Vermont
Vital Records Section, Department of Health
www.sover.net/~mbevins/birth.htm

Virginia
Department of Health
www.vdh.state.va.us/misc/gene.htm
The Library of Virginia has copies of surviving birth and death records for the period 1853 to 1896 and marriage records prior to 1936. Visit the Library of Virginia's web site at
http://www.vdh.state.va.us/misc/gene.htm

Washington
Department of Health, Center for Health Statistics
http://vitalrec.com/wa.html

West Virginia
Division of Health, Vital Registration
www.wvdhhr.org/bph/oehp/hsc/vr/birtcert.htm

Wisconsin
Division of Health, Vital Records
http://www.dhfs.state.wi.us/vitalrecords/index.htm

Wyoming
Vital Records Services
http://wdhfs.state.wy.us/vital_records/

Filing the Documents

As you receive documents through the mail, you need to file them (or copies of them) along with your notes in a notebook. One notebook can be organized by the surname of the ancestor; and as more records are added, you can separate the notes and documents by the places people lived. For example, you could have one notebook on the Johnson families (plus people who married into the Johnson family), then separate the Iowa Johnson notes in one group, the Kansas Johnson notes in another group, and so on.

Summary — Get the Vital Records

Step four in the process of finding your ancestors is the gathering of vital records for parents, grandparents, etc. After you obtain a death certificate, there are several other possible records relating to a person's death that may add much more information. These records come from funeral homes, cemeteries, obituaries, social security records, and other death records. All of these death records should be obtained for every member of a family, including the brothers and sisters of your ancestors. Birth, marriage, and divorce records should be obtained for every member of a family as well.

Genealogists enjoy the quiet, serene atmosphere of their local library as a place for research.

Search the Census Records

Why Census Records?

Uncle Sam has been in the business of taking censuses in the U.S. since 1790. Every ten years, comprehensive lists of names of people are given in census records. For every census from 1790 through 1840, the names of nearly all of the heads of household living in America were recorded. And, for every ten-year period from 1850 through 1920, the names of nearly every single person who lived in this country were recorded. Most of these census name lists still exist. As a result, census records are, by far, the greatest American name-finding resource available to genealogists.

Census research also reveals the exact place in the United States where a person lived. There is much that can be learned about your ancestors in census records. But, just learning where your ancestor lived can be the clue you may need to find where even more written records are stored today. So, we use the censuses to locate the county of residence for an ancestor, record everything we can from the censuses, then move on to resources available in that particular county. A county courthouse is a treasure chest of genealogical information. To get there, we need the censuses to put us in the right county.

Dates and Places Needed First

Your first collected genealogical facts were gathered from home sources; interviews with relatives; and vital records, such as death certificates. Based on what you learned in the first gathering of facts, the next step is a search in the U.S. federal censuses for your ancestors. An understanding of the dates and places where your people lived will be the clue to accessing the census records to use first. For example, if a death certificate reveals the place of birth of your grandfather as Alabama in 1911, that information should lead you to a written account in which your grandfather appears as a 9-year-old child in a family identified in the 1920 federal census. The key piece of information you would need to know to find this census record is the fact that the person lived in Alabama. As it turns out, if you know the place a person lived in the U.S. any time between 1790 and 1920, you have a very good chance of finding them in a census. All names recorded in census records are organized by the places people live, such as a rural postal route, voting precinct, school district, township, village, town, or city. In all censuses, these places are organized under a county, and then the counties are gathered together for each U.S. state or territory. So, finding the state or territory where an ancestor lived is the starting point for census research. The people listed in the censuses are easy to find, because most of the decennial censuses have statewide name indexes.

Although there is a federal privacy law restricting information in a census for 72 years, the censuses from 1790 through 1920 are open to the public. So, a researcher can browse through census records looking for Abraham Lincoln, Jesse James, or an ancestor who was in the Poor House in Boston in 1850. Genealogists are looking forward to the opening of the 1930 census which the National Archives has already announced will happen on 1 April 2002.

Who's in the Censuses?

The first five censuses, 1790-1840, recorded only the names of the heads of households living in every state and numbers within age categories for males and females included in a particular household. Even with just the names of heads of households shown, these census lists are valuable finding aids. Virtually all of the early census name lists have been indexed in book form for each state or as CD-ROM publications.

Genealogy Rule #18:
A census record showing all twelve children in a family proves only that your ancestors did not believe in birth control.

Beginning in 1850, the censuses were recorded by listing the names of every member of a household making the federal census schedules from 1850 forward tremendous sources for finding entire families living in America.

The name lists from the 1850-1870 censuses have all been indexed in book form for all states or as CD-ROM publications. Special name indexes to the 1880-1920 censuses also exist, either as individual state publications, or as Soundex indexes.

A majority of the old census name lists survive for all censuses except 1890 (which was mostly destroyed after a fire in 1921) and several states from 1790-1830. Most of the surviving original manuscripts of the early censuses, 1790-1880, are now located in the National Archives in Washington, D.C. All of the early censuses have been microfilmed. The censuses taken for 1900, 1910, and 1920 were microfilmed; but the originals were destroyed.

Soundex Indexes

The first Soundex indexes were originally prepared by the Works Progress Administration (WPA) in the late 1930's as an aid to finding evidence of a person's age. With the advent of Social Security in 1935, an index was needed to quickly access the census schedules and provide people with proof of age in lieu of a birth certificate. Thus, the Soundex system was created which was used to index all or parts of the 1880, 1900, 1920, and 1930 censuses. A partial Soundex index to the 1910 census was also done by the Census Bureau's Age Search Group in the early 1960's.

As the latest census open to the public until the year 2002, the 1920 census is the first place to start searching federal census records for your recent ancestors; and the 1920 Soundex is the tool for locating a family.

Start With the 1920 Soundex Index

A rule in genealogy is to "work from the known to the unknown." Skipping generations is a no-no. Therefore, census research should be done by starting with the latest census with the best chance of finding an ancestor, and then working back in time, in ten-year intervals, to the earlier censuses.

Genealogy Rule #19:
Work from the known to the unknown. In other words, just because your name is Washington doesn't mean you are related to George.

Following this rule, the starting point for census research for most genealogists is the name index (Soundex) to the 1920 census. The 1920 Soundex, an extraction from the full 1920 census schedules, indexes every head of household in America in 1920. It was originally recorded on thousands of 3"x 5" index cards. All of the cards were microfilmed, and the Soundex indexes are now available on rolls of microfilm located at many libraries and archives across the country.

Once a head of household's name is found on one of the Soundex index cards, any other household members are also named, along with their ages, places of birth, and their relationship to the head of the house. Thus, the 1920 Soundex is not an every-name index, but virtually every name appears on the Soundex cards.

Even without knowing the full name of the head of household, locating a child in a family in the 1920 Soundex is possible. Let's say you have a death certificate for your grandfather who was born in Alabama in 1911. You know his name was John Henry Johnson and that he would have been nine years old in 1920 and was probably living with his parents somewhere in Alabama. But let's assume that the names of John Henry Johnson's father and mother, your great-grandparents, are not known.

A search of the Soundex cards for Alabama and the surname Johnson can be done, looking for any male or female head of household named Johnson with a 9-year-old John Henry Johnson shown as a child in the family. There may have been dozens of heads of household named Johnson in Alabama in 1920, but searching the Soundex cards is not as difficult as it may seem. It is a matter of looking at each card until you find the name of a child that matches what you know which should then reveal the names of the parents. If you know the first names of brothers or sisters of the child you are looking for, that will provide even more confirmation that you have the correct family; and you will have discovered the names of the child's father and mother.

If a child in the 1920 Soundex were not living with his parents, but with another family with a different surname, the child will appear on a separate index card as if he were a head of household. Thus, any person with a different surname than the head of household can be found in the main Soundex listing.

After locating a family in the 1920 Soundex, the full census schedules can be consulted. Each Soundex card provides the information needed to access the census schedules, i.e., the Enumeration District number, the census page number, and the line number of the page. The Soundex cards were copied from the full census schedules and show a person's relationship to the head of house. Rather than a strict alphabetical order, the cards are organized by the Soundex code for a surname, followed by the first name of the head of household.

The information on the Soundex cards are secondary sources. There are many instances of copying errors on the Soundex cards, such as different spelling of names, wrong ages, and incorrect places of birth. The census schedules are the primary sources for collecting information about your families. So, it is important that we use the Soundex cards, but only as a means to locate a family in the census schedules.

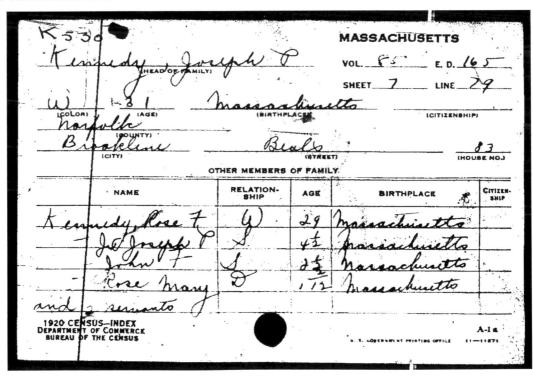

1920 Soundex Index Card. Taken from the 1920 census schedules, these cards were created by clerical workers of the WPA in the late 1930s. The index card indicates a head of household and all other persons in a household.

Soundex Coding System

A Soundex coding system is a method of indexing surnames by removing all vowels and extra letters, and then coding the hard sounds of the remaining letters. This indexing system allows you to find a person in the census whose surname can be spelled different ways.

As an example, a listing of the heads of households with the surname Cooley, Couley, Cooly, Couly, or Coolley would all appear under the Soundex Code C400, then alphabetically by their first names, as shown below:

Soundex
Code	Surname, first name
C400	Couley, Abraham
C400	Cooley, Bradley
C400	Coolley, Charles
C400	Cooly, David
C400	Couly, Elmer

How to Code a Surname

Code	Key letters and equivalents
1	b, p, f, v
2	c, s, k, g, j, q, x, z
3	d, t
4	l
5	m, n
6	r

The first letter of a surname is not coded, and the letters a, e, i, o, u, y, w, and h are not coded. Also, any two or more letters together with the same code are coded as one letter. For example, if the letters c-s appear together (as in the name Tri**cs**e) they are coded as one letter, or if the letters c-s-k appear together (as in Coussa**csk**), they are coded as one letter. In both cases, the code for c-s or c-s-k would be the number 2.

Every Soundex code number must be four characters: a first letter of a surname, followed by three numerical digits. A name yielding all vowels after the first letter, such as Lee, would thus be L000. A name yielding only one code number would have two zeros added, such as Kuhne, coded as K500. A name yielding only two code letters would have one zero added, as Ebell, coded as E140. Not more than three number digits are used, so Ebelson would be coded as E142, not E1425.

Soundex Generator Programs

To find out what the Soundex Code is for any surname, use the Internet site shown below. This web page has an automatic and instant Soundex generator, based on any name you type, and includes a good explanation of the Soundex coding system:
http://www.frontiernet.net/~rjacob/soundex.htm

As a backup, two other web sites will calculate a Soundex code for any surname:
http://searches.rootsweb.com/cgi-bin/Genea/soundex.sh
http://www.nara.gov/genealogy/soundex/soundex.html

Census Availability

1790-1820. All the surviving census originals from 1790-1820 were microfilmed, and the surviving manuscripts are still stored at the National Archives. However, it is in the first four censuses where the most losses have occurred, with several statewide losses. The statewide losses are shown in the list below.

1830-1870. All states and territories from 1830-1870 have complete censuses which survive and have been microfilmed. The original manuscripts are located at the National Archives.

1880. After they were microfilmed, the original 1880 census schedules for all states were transferred to various universities, archives, state libraries, DAR library, or other repositories around the country. This was the only census that was handled in this way.

1890. Over 99% of the 1890 census was destroyed as a result of a disastrous fire which took place in the Commerce Building in Washington, D.C. in 1921, well before any of the censuses were microfilmed.

1900-1940. After the 1900 through 1940 census schedules were microfilmed, the original manuscripts were destroyed.

Statewide Census Losses

1790. Delaware, Georgia, New Jersey, and Virginia (including present-day Kentucky and West Virginia). All of these states have had census substitutes published, with the list of names taken from tax lists, voter registrations, or other county records.

1800. Georgia, Illinois Territory, Indiana Territory, Kentucky, Mississippi Territory, New Jersey, and Tennessee.

1810. District of Columbia, Georgia, Indiana Territory, Michigan Territory, Mississippi Territory, New Jersey, and Tennessee.

1820. Alabama, Arkansas Territory, Missouri Territory, and New Jersey.

1890. Most of the census schedules were destroyed during or after a fire in 1921. A total of 6,106 names was extracted from the surviving fragments of the census schedules, representing less than 1/10 of 1% of the U.S. population of about 63 million people in 1890.

Where are the Microfilmed Census Records?

The following is a list of the major genealogical research facilities in the U.S., particularly those with complete microfilm sets of the U.S. Federal Census Schedules, 1790-1920; all Soundex Indexes on microfilm, 1880-1920; and most published census indexes.

- **History Library,** Salt Lake City, Utah. This is the world's largest genealogical library and has all census microfilm, 1790-1920, and most published census indexes. In addition to the Salt Lake facility, there are more than 2,000 branch libraries in the U.S. (Family History Centers) where microfilm can be borrowed from the Salt Lake facility and used at a local branch. Searchable databases, the complete library catalog, and a list of locations and phone numbers for the U.S. Family History Centers can be found at the Family History Library's Internet site: www.familysearch.org.

- **Heritage Quest,** North Salt Lake, Utah, a lending library, with the largest commercial collection of genealogical data in America. Members can borrow rolls of microfilm for 30 days; or anyone can purchase digitized versions on CD-ROM for all federal censuses, 1790-1920. A complete catalog of census films and digital microfilm versions can be found at their Internet site: www.heritagequest.com

- **Allen County Public Library,** Fort Wayne, Indiana. One of the largest genealogical collections in the country, and with all census film, 1790-1920. A complete catalog of their holdings can be found at their Internet site: www.acpl.lib.in.us/genealogy/genealogy.html

- **Mid-Continent Library,** Independence, Missouri. This regional library has an outstanding collection of genealogical materials and includes all census film, 1790-1920. A description of their holdings and hours of operations can be found at their Internet site: www.mcpl.lib.mo.us/

- **State Historical Society of Wisconsin,** Madison, Wisconsin. The genealogy collection is very large and includes all federal census film, 1790-1920. Descriptions of their holdings can be found at their Internet site: www.shsw.wisc.edu/library/index.html.

- **Public Library of Cincinnati and Hamilton County, Cincinnati, Ohio.** The genealogy collection is very large and includes all fedcral census film, 1790-1920. Descriptions of their holding can be found at their Internet site: http://plch.lib.oh.us/

- **National Archives Reference Branch, Archives I,** National Archives and Records Administration, Washington, D.C. This is the main downtown Washington branch, with a microfilm reading room for viewing all of the censuses. This is where the surviving original census manuscripts from 1790-1880 are stored. Details about censuses can be found at their Internet site: www.nara.gov/.

■ **Regional Records Services Facilities** of the National Archives and Records Administration. Thirteen of these regional facilities have complete sets of all censuses 1790-1920 on microfilm, and each has public reading rooms. Their locations and Internet addresses are given below, where one can find their street addresses, phone numbers, and hours of operation:

- Northeast Region (**Boston**), National Archives and Records Administration, Waltham, Massachusetts.
www.nara.gov/regional/boston.html

- Northeast Region (**Pittsfield**), National Archives and Records Administration, Pittsfield, Massachusetts.
www.nara.gov/regional/pittsfie.html

- Northeast Region (**New York City**), National Archives and Records Administration, New York, New York.
www.nara.gov/regional/newyork.html

- Mid-Atlantic Region (**Philadelphia Center City**), National Archives and Records Administration, Philadelphia, Pennsylvania.
www.nara.gov/regional/philacc.html

- Southeast Region (**Atlanta**), National Archives and Records Administration, East Point, Geogia.
www.nara.gov/regional/atlanta.html

- Great Lakes Region (**Chicago**), National Archives and Records Administration, Chicago, Illinois. www.nara.gov/regional/chicago.html

- Central Plains Region (**Kansas City**), National Archives and Records Administration, Kansas City, Missouri.
www.nara.gov/regional/kansas.html

- Southwest Region (**Fort Worth**), National Archives and Records Administration, Fort Worth, Texas.
www.nara.gov/regional/ftworth.html

- Rocky Mountain Region (**Denver**), National Archives and Records Administration. Denver, Colorado.
www.nara.gov/regional/denver.html

- Pacific Region (**Laguna Niguel**), National Archives and Records Administration, Laguna Niguel, California.
www.nara.gov/regional/laguna.html

- Pacific Region (**San Francisco**), National Archives and Records Administration, San Bruno, California.
www.nara.gov/regional/sanfranc.html

- Pacific Alaska Region (Seattle), National Archives and Records Administration, Seattle, Washington.
www.nara.gov/regional/seattle.html

- Pacific Alaska Region (**Anchorage**), National Archives and Records Administration, Anchorage, Alaska.
www.nara.gov/regional/anchorag.html

Search the Internet for Census Records

The Internet has become a source to find and view historical documents. Federal censuses, for example, have been transcribed and made available on the Internet as scanned digitized images of the census documents, extracted typescripts, or as indexes to the names of heads of households.

All census records, 1790-1920 are now available on the Internet at the Heritage Quest site: www.genealogydatabase.com. Subscribers may access any page of the censuses and print facsimile pages of the originals at home.

USGenWeb Census Project

Access this web site at http://www.rootsweb.com/~usgenweb/census/ The USGenWeb Census Project was started in February 1997 with the mission of transcribing all of the US Federal Censuses for free access by anyone. It's an ambitious project with volunteer genealogists participating in the transcription and/or indexing of names from all of the federal censuses, 1790-1920. So far, less than five percent of the censuses have been transcribed and made available on the Internet, but this project is ongoing and promises to complete all states for all census years, 1790-1920. The US GenWeb Census Project is linked to the Heritage Quest site for viewing all census records online.

To search for already transcribed census information, the **On-Line Inventory of Transcribed Census Links** lists the files completed by Census Project volunteers. This list is updated weekly.

The **State Census Status** pages list the current county transcriber assignment status. For example, there is an 1850 Baldwin County, Alabama census transcription and index, which can be viewed on screen. This index gives a person's first and last name, and a reference to the census page, microfilm series number and roll number. In addition, the text from each page of the 1850 Baldwin County federal census has been transcribed.

Cyndi's List — Census Related Sites

A good place to find genealogy Internet sites is www.cyndislist.com. Over 80,000 web-sites are categorized, including several sites related to censuses. Use Cyndi's List to find web sites related to the census, such as:

- General Resource Sites
- Printable Census Forms
- Publications, Software & Supplies
- Soundex
- U.S. Census Indexes & Records
- USGenWeb Archives Census Project
- Census Related Sites Worldwide
- U.S. — National Archives

Heritage Quest Digital Archives

Heritage Quest of North Salt Lake, Utah has digitized the images of all census records, 1790-1920. The scanned images are organized exactly the same as for one roll of microfilm and a genealogist can order a CD-ROM containing the contents of any federal census, using the same microfilm series number and roll number. The price for one CD-ROM disk is less than for purchasing a roll of film from the National Archives.

A complete review and ordering information for the Digital Archives program can be found at their web site: www.heritagequest.com.

Published Census Indexes

Published statewide census indexes exist for all U.S. states and territories for the censuses taken from 1790 through 1870. Most of the indexes are for the heads of household, but a few are "every-name" indexes, which include the names of every person listed in a particular household.

The largest source for the census indexes, 1790-1860 are those produced on CD-ROM by Broderbund, the publisher of Family Tree Maker software. Their indexes are identified and available for purchase at their web site: www.familytreemaker.com.

In addition, all of the 1790, 1800, 1810, and 1870 federal censuses have been indexed by Heritage Quest. See the complete list at their web-site: www.heritagequest.com.

Summary — Search the Census Records

Uncle Sam has been in the business of taking censuses in the U.S. since 1790. Every ten years, comprehensive lists of names of people are found in census records. For every census from 1790 through 1840, the names of nearly all of the heads of household in America were recorded. And, for every ten-year period from 1850 through 1920, the names of nearly every single person who lived in this country were recorded. Most of these census name lists still exist. As a result, census records are, by far, the greatest American name-finding resource available to genealogists.

Census research also reveals the exact place on the ground where a person lived. There is much that can be learned about your ancestors in census records, but just learning where an ancestor lived in a certain time period can be all the clues you may need to find where even more written records are stored today. So, we use the censuses to locate the county of residence for an ancestor, record everything we can from the censuses, then move onto resources available in that particular county. A county courthouse is a treasure chest of genealogical information. To get there, we need the censuses to put us in the right county.

Step 6

Search the Local and State Sources

Genealogy Rule #20:
A good genealogical source record is any document that confirms that your ancestor was from this planet.

Local Genealogical Source Records

It is local government which has the most direct contact with people's lives. Although we all pay federal income tax, vote in national elections, and use state or federal government services — the place where your names can be found most frequently is in documents found at the local level of government. A typical county courthouse contains a treasure chest of genealogical information about the residents of that county, past and present. In the New England states, a town hall may contain the same type of genealogical treasures.

For example, your birth, marriage, or divorce records are first recorded at the town or county level of government. In most states, your local property taxes are collected and recorded by a county tax assessor. If you ever brought a lawsuit against someone, the civil court records for the case are still there in the county courthouse. Criminals brought to justice are handled mostly in county courts, and probate records relating to the property of a deceased person are usually found in a county courthouse.

In addition to records found in a town hall or county courthouse, other local sources in a county, such as those found in libraries, museums, funeral homes, cemeteries, churches, etc., are the ones with the best chance of providing evidence of a person's birth, marriage, residence, or death at a certain place. As the facts about a person's life are recorded in these local facilities, the recorded facts become genealogical source records.

The local authorities who created these records do not refer to them as "genealogical source records," and none of these records were created for the convenience of family historians. Sources at the county level all had an original purpose, such as recording the names of people living in a area, burials in a cemetery, or keeping track of land owners, taxpayers, probates, etc.

Most of these records were compiled in the order they were first created. Names of people found in a county tax list, for example, are rarely listed in alphabetical order. Instead, local records are logically organized by the place and date of the records. So, after learning the *place* where an ancestor lived, knowing *when* an ancestor lived there is the next pointer and will lead to success in finding and using local genealogical source records.

Find the Place   Find the Facts

Until now, your genealogical research has involved the use of home sources, relatives, vital records, and census records. The research tools you have used so far will help you find the places where your ancestors lived. It is now time to discover the vast quantity of genealogical reference material that is available at these places.

For example, specific facts discovered on a death certificate — such as the places of birth for your great-grandparents — are important clues to finding more data. And, places identified after using the 1920 census to locate the places your ancestors lived will lead you to more possibilities for genealogical references. What is the best way to find genealogical references available for one U.S. county? Do you have to visit that county in person?

Let's Go to Baldwin County, Alabama

Let's say the 1920 census records lead you to Baldwin County, Alabama, as the place where an ancestor lived. If so, the local records created and maintained in Baldwin County will now present the best opportunity for discovering more genealogical evidence. Therefore, a survey is now needed to tell you what kinds of historical records may exist for Baldwin County.

One way to conduct this survey would be to fly to Mobile Regional Airport, rent a car, drive east across Mobile Bay on Interstate 10 to exit 38, and then drive north about 15 miles to the town of Bay Minette (the county seat of Baldwin County). Get a motel room, check out one of the local diners, and then spend whatever time is necessary there to work on the survey. All you need to take with you is a pencil, a notepad, a cell-phone, and a Visa card.

While there, you should try to learn which Baldwin County office is in charge of different types of records. Find out where you can find the Baldwin County Health Department, a local source for Alabama birth and death records (since 1908) through the statewide health network. You should also learn which Baldwin county office has older birth and death records; marriage records; land records, probate records, civil court records, and criminal court records. And, you should learn if any of these old court records have been transferred out of the county courthouse or moved to the State Archives (You may have to drive to Montgomery next.) It would also be worthwhile to determine if any of the old court records have been microfilmed.

In addition to the court records in Bay Minette, you can find out about the local cemeteries, funeral homes, museums, historical societies, genealogical societies, and maybe even find a person who is into genealogy and lives there — genealogists love to show off their home town and resources. For any published histories of the region, you can go visit the public library in Bay Minette or the college library at the University of South Alabama, Baldwin County, located just a few miles south of town.

You could do all these things by personally visiting and surveying the places where your ancestors lived. In most cases, visiting the place in person is the best way to learn what genealogical resources are located there.

However, sometimes the historical source records are no longer located at a county courthouse or town hall, but have been removed for safekeeping to a larger facility, such as a library or archives. You also may discover that many of the old county records have been microfilmed, and copies are available at sites outside of the area.

But wait! You may be able to do many of these local survey tasks without having to travel to the place. In fact, if your computer is connected to the Internet, you can start the place survey without leaving home!

Survey the Family History Library

Before heading out to each of the locations where your ancestors lived, first use the resources of the world's largest genealogical library — the **Family History Library**™ in Salt Lake City, Utah. Branches of the main library are called Family History Centers™, and there over 3,000 branches worldwide. There may be one very near your place of residence.

The Family History Library (FHL) has over two million rolls of microfilm, over 400,000 books, and ranks as one of the largest libraries of any kind in the country. Owned and operated by The Church of Jesus Christ of Latter-day Saints (LDS), the library is open to anyone interested in genealogy.

Genealogy Rule #21:
The Mormon Library in Salt Lake City is a great place for genealogical research... but, the only Mormons you will find at the library work there.

Although the library has thousands of published family histories related to many different surnames and family lines, the vast majority of the collection is made up of historic manuscripts (on microfilm) from local, state, or national jurisdictions around the world. For example, nearly every county in the U.S. is represented with original court records on microfilm, including births, deaths, marriages, censuses, tax lists, deeds, wills, probates, and more.

For American resources, just about everything a genealogist will find at the Family History Library could be obtained by contacting a county courthouse, state library, or state or national archives. But nowhere else can you jump from county to county or state to state, to locate your ancestors in historical records — all in the same building.

Types of FHL Sources

The Family History Library has several different types of local genealogical sources, most of which are in the form of historical manuscripts on microfilm. A great number of these references are records from American counties. The types of genealogical source records on microfilm at the Family History

Library and specific to a particular U.S. county may include the following:

- Vital Records: births, marriages, divorces, deaths, and burials.

- Court Records: probate records, including administrations, estate settlements, wills, names of heirs, etc.; civil court records; and criminal court records.

- First Papers and other naturalization records. Those initiated at the county level.

- Military records: militia lists or copies of veterans discharge papers.

- Assessment lists: county-wide lists of taxpayers for a particular year.

- Censuses. state or federal censuses listing names of inhabitants of the county.

- Voter registration lists.

- Land and Property Records: recorded deeds (showing names of buyers and sellers of land); land grants and real estate records, such as mortgages, liens, sheriff sales; and land ownership maps and atlases.

- Registrations: cattle brands, business, and professional licenses.

- Histories: books or articles specific to the history of a certain place. Names of early settlers, businesses, schoolteachers, politicians, etc., are often found in county histories.

- Cemeteries and Funeral Homes: list of burials, locations, and maps.

- Church records: membership lists, births, christenings, baptisms, marriages, deaths, and burials recorded at local churches.

- Genealogical and historical society publications.

Many of the microfilmed genealogical source records are from the United States; but the Family History Library also has large collections of source materials from Canada, England, Wales, Scotland, Ireland, Germany, and the Scandinavian countries. Many other countries are well represented as well. It is said that an American researcher with Mexican ancestors can accomplish more genealogy in Salt Lake City than by traveling to Mexico. (Catholic christening records from virtually every parish in Mexico have been microfilmed by the Genealogical Society of Utah, an independent corporation of The Church of Jesus Christ of Latter-day Saints (LDS).

Branch Libraries Too!

The Family History Library (FHL) in Salt Lake City serves as a lending agent to over 3,600 branch libraries around the world, called Family History Centers. Just about any microfilmed resource that can be found at the Salt Lake facility can be borrowed and used at one of the branches. With only a few exceptions, all Family History Centers are located within an LDS church building, located all over the country. All of them are open to the public.

As it turns out, the Family History Library and any of its many branches provide a one-stop service to genealogists. They can be used to determine what resources may be available for genealogical research in a particular area of the world, or for a specific family line. The Family History Library Catalog is a tremendous tool for genealogical research, because you can search the contents of the largest collection of genealogical source material in one place — containing more than any other library or archives in the country.

The FamilySearch™ System

The Family History Library Catalog is included in the FHL computer "look-up" system, called **FamilySearch**™ Also included in this very sophisticated computer file are the International Genealogical Index™ (IGI) and the Ancestral File,™ which together contain over 360 million names from all over the world.

The FamilySearch system is distributed on CD-ROM to all of the Family History Centers where a name or place search on a computer can be conducted in person. Even better, the Family History Library's FamilySearch system is now available on the Internet at www.FamilySearch.com. A complete list of the Family History Centers with their addresses and phone numbers can be found at the FamilySearch Internet site along with many other features including a search for the names of your ancestors.

Survey the FHL Sources for a Place

The first place to start in the Family History Library is the catalog, because you need to identify genealogical source records found in local, and state repositories. In particular, you need to survey the FHL catalog for the places where your ancestors lived.

Here is an example of finding local genealogical source records from Baldwin County, Alabama. Using the Family History Library's Internet website at www.familysearch.com, a search of the on-line catalog would reveal that there are 15 topics relating to Baldwin County, Alabama:

Place: Alabama, Baldwin

Notes: Baldwin County was created by act of the Mississippi territorial legislature on 21 December 1809. Parent county was Washington and part of Florida. County seat: McIntosh Bluff on the Tombigbee (1809-1820), Blakeley (1820-1868), Daphne (1868-1901), and Bay Minette (October 1901-present).

Topics:
    Alabama, Baldwin - Cemeteries
    Alabama, Baldwin - Census - 1820
    Alabama, Baldwin - Census - 1855
    Alabama, Baldwin - Census - 1855
    Alabama, Baldwin - Census - 1860
    Alabama, Baldwin - Census - 1866
    Alabama, Baldwin - Census - 1870
    Alabama, Baldwin - Court records
    Alabama, Baldwin - Court records - Indexes
    Alabama, Baldwin - History
    Alabama, Baldwin - Land and property
    Alabama, Baldwin - Maps
    Alabama, Baldwin - Probate records
    Alabama, Baldwin - Vital records

Each of the 15 topics listed above can be reviewed in more detail, for example, moving to the next level under the topic, Alabama, Baldwin - Land and property, would reveal the following titles:

Topic: Alabama, Baldwin - Land and property
Titles:
- Deeds, 1809-1901; indexes, 1905-1925, Alabama. Probate Court (Baldwin County)
- Deeds, 1836-1897 , Alabama. Probate Court (Baldwin County)
- Land atlas and plat book, Baldwin County, Alabama, Rockford Map Publishers
- Mobile land grants, 1710-1795, Andrews, Johnnie

Each of the above titles can be seen at the next level, for example, the one entitled, Deeds, 1809-1901; indexes, 1905-1925 , Alabama. Probate Court (Baldwin County) would be described as follows:

    Subject: Alabama, Baldwin - Land and Property

    Title: Deeds, 1809-1901; indexes, 1905-1925 Probate Court
    Notes: Microfilm of originals in the Baldwin County courthouse in Bay Minette, Alabama. Some
        pages wanting, faded, torn, bleeding through, etc.
    Format: Manuscript (On Film)
    Language: English.
    Publication: Salt Lake City: Filmed by the Genealogical Society of Utah, 1992.
    Physical: on 7 microfilm reels; 35 mm.

Finally, one can go one more level and review the film titles and film numbers for the seven rolls of microfilm relating to <u>Deeds, 1809-1901; indexes, 1905-1925 Probate Court</u>:

Alabama, Baldwin - Land and Property

Title: <u>Deeds, 1809-1901; indexes, 1905-1925 Probate Court</u>

Microfilm Reels:
1. General deed index direct A-Krz 1905-1925. Film #1838847, item 2.
2. General deed index direct Lae-XYZ 1905-1925. Film #1838964
3. Deeds v. A-C 1809-1835. Film #1838967, items 2-4.
4. Deeds v. Y-Z (p. 1-408) 1898-1899. #Film 1839366.
5. Deeds v. Z (p. 409-end) 1899. Film #1839367, item 1.
6. Deeds v. 1 - 2 (p. 1-426) 1899-1900. Film #1839367, items 2-3..
7. Deeds v. 2 (p. 426-end) -v. 3 (ns) 1900-1901. Film #1839368.

Looking at each of the 15 topics for Baldwin County in this way would reveal that the Family History Library has several books and over 100 rolls of microfilm specific to that county. Each roll of microfilm is equivalent to a 300 page book. The Baldwin County, Alabama, example can be repeated for every county in the U.S. where a survey of genealogical source material is desired.

Survey the State Archives

The example of the survey work to locate Baldwin County historical records in the Family History Library Catalog can be repeated in the catalog of the Alabama state archives. Located in Montgomery, the Alabama Department of Archives and History (ADAH) is an outstanding center for genealogical research in Alabama historical sources. This is true for genealogical research in the state archives for all U.S. states, but the state archives in the southern states are generally very good at catering to and providing historical records specifically for genealogical researchers.

Like most of the state archives, the Alabama state archives has an Internet website. So, with your computer and an Internet connection, you can get an overview of what types of historical records can be found for the state of Alabama and for all Alabama counties. For example, the ADAH website features a "Family History and Genealogy " section, where you can find a list of microfilmed records relating to all Alabama counties, including Baldwin County. Here is an overview of genealogical source records found at the ADAH website:

Family History and Genealogy - Categories

- Federal Census
- State Census
- County Records (deeds, wills, & other probate records)
- Vital Records (birth, death, marriage, & divorce)

- Land Records
- Military Records
- Military Discharge records
- Surname Files
- City Directories
- African-American
- Native American
- Immigration and Naturalization
- Historical & Genealogical Societies
- Related Links
- Genealogy Records not at the ADAH
- Newspapers

Examples of the details for some of the items on the above list of categories are show below. Selecting "County Records" from the list, for example, would bring up a complete list of all Alabama counties for selecting details. Selecting "Baldwin County" would reveal a good representation of the historical records available as shown below:

Baldwin County
- **County Records** (on microfilm):
  - Will records, 1809-1909
  - Direct Index to Probate records, 1810-1925
  - Direct Index to Deeds, 1905-1935
  - Reverse Index to Deeds, 1810-1911
  - Deed Records, 1809-1901
  - General Index to Orphans Court and Probate Court records, 1820-1930
  - Orphans Court records, 1822-1854
  - Probate Court records, 1855-1929
  - Orphans Court minutes, 1822-1856
  - Probate Court minutes, 1850-1928
  - Tax Assessor, assessment record of personal property, 1849
- **Vital Records** (on Microfilm):
  - Birth and Death Records, 1886-1919
  - Marriage Records (Colored), 1896-1935
  - Marriage Records (White), 1810-1836
- **Original Vital Records at:**
  - County Clerk
    Baldwin County Courthouse
    PO Box 459
    Bay Minette, AL 36507
    Phone: (334) 937-0260
    Fax: (334) 580-2563
- **Newspapers** (on Microfilm):
  - *The American Banner* (Bay Minette), Sept. 16, 1899 - Feb. 1, 1902.
  - *The Baldwin Times* (Daphne), May 21, 1896 - Dec. 28, 1998.

- *Eastern Shore Courier* (Fairhope), Sept. 2, 1927 - Sept. 29, 1993.
- *The Fairhope Courier* (Fairhope), Mar., 1901 - Sept., 1995.
- *The Independent* (Robertsdale), Jan. 6, 1982 - June 29, 1995.
- *The Onlooker* (Foley), Jan. 14, 1910 - Aug. 30, 1995
- **History:**

Baldwin County was created by the Mississippi territorial legislature on Dec. 21, 1809 from territory taken from Washington County. Its size was altered several times before 1868 when it received its present dimensions. Baldwin County lies in the southwestern part of the state. It is bounded on the north by Clarke and Monroe Counties, on the east by Escambia County, AL, and Escambia County, FL, on the west by Clarke, Washington, and Mobile counties, and Mobile Bay, and on the south by the Gulf of Mexico. It was named for Abraham Baldwin, a distinguished citizen of Georgia. MacIntosh Bluff, Blakeley, and Daphne each served for a time as county seat before 1901, when Bay Minette was so designated. Other towns and communities include: Bon Secour, Elberta, Fairhope, Foley, Lillian, Loxley, Perdido Beach, Point Clear, Robertsdale, Summerdale, and Gulf Shores. Authority: Owen, Thomas McAdory. *History of Alabama and Dictionary of Alabama Biography*. Chicago: S.J. Clarke Publishing Co., 1921.

- **Historical and Genealogical Societies:**
  - Baldwin County Historical Society
    PO Box 69
    Stockton, AL 36579
  - Baldwin County Genealogical Society
    c/o Foley Public Library
    319 East Laurel Ave.
    Foley, AL 36535
    Publication: Yore Lore
    Website: http://www.rootsweb.com/~albaldwi/index.html or
    http://www.gulftel.net/bcgs

Cyndi's List On The Internet

To find out what genealogical resources may be available on the Internet, go first to www.cyndislist.com, a categorized list of over 80,000 web sites related to genealogy. As an example of what you may find for one state, the alphabetized categories under "**Alabama**" are listed below:

- General Resource Sites
- Government & Cities
- History & Culture
- Libraries, Archives & Museums
- Mailing Lists, Newsgroups & Chat
- Maps, Gazetteers & Geographical Information
- Military
- Newspapers
- People & Families
- Professional Researchers, Volunteers & Other Research Services

Step 6: Search the Local and State Sources

- Publications, Software & Supplies
- Queries, Message Boards & Surname Lists
- Records: Census, Cemeteries, Land, Obituaries, Personal, Taxes, and Vital Records (**see category list below**)
- Religion & Churches
- Societies & Groups
- U.S. — Counties, Localities and Regions

The sites found in each of the above categories vary in content. Some sites have extractions or transcriptions of actual records. Other sites have helpful lists, articles, tips, or guidelines. In a few cases there are scanned images of the original source documents themselves, with more of these types of records coming online each day.

As an example of just one of the above categories, **Records: Census, Cemeteries, Land, Obituaries, Personal, Taxes and Vital Records**, a detailed list of source references relating to Alabama records can be found. Each of the sites are hot-linked so a user can go directly to that Internet site.

- The 1790-1890 Federal Population Censuses: Catalog of National Archives Microfilm Census Schedules and Microfilm Roll Numbers for Alabama: 1830, 1840, 1850, 1860, 1870, 1880, 1880 Soundex
- 1809 Census of Madison County Alabama
- Some transcriptions of Tuscaloosa County cemeteries
- African American Cemeteries Online - Alabama
- African American Census Schedules Online - Alabama
- Alabama Department of Public Health - How to Obtain Birth and Death Certificates
- Alabama Live Obituary Listing (Birmingham, Huntsville, Mobile)
- Alabama Marriages Indexed by Grooms Name Mobile and Wilcox Counties
- Alabama Territorial Records
- Alabama Vital Records Information
- Alabama Wedding Bells
- Post marriages that took place prior to 1900
- Autauga County, Alabama 1830 Census
- Autauga County, Alabama 1840 Census
- Autauga County, Alabama Cemetery Listings
- Autauga County, Alabama Super Index
- Search a consolidated index of Autauga County resources compiled by Larry Nobles
- Blount County, Alabama 1830 Census
- The Bureau of Land Management - Eastern States, General Land Office, the official Land Patent Records site. This site has a searchable database of over two million pre-1908 Federal land title records, including scanned images of those records. The Eastern Public Land States covered in this database are: Alabama, Arkansas, Florida, Illinois, Indiana, Louisiana, Michigan, Minnesota, Mississippi, Missouri, Ohio, Wisconsin
- Cemeteries of the United States - Alabama Cemeteries - County Index
- CensusLinks - Alabama

- Census of Madison County (Alabama) Mississippi Territory Taken January 1809
- Census Online - Links to Census Sites on the Web - Alabama
- Chilton Cemeteries. Includes: Bethany Missionary Baptist Church, Bethel Primitive Baptist Church, Bethsalem Baptist Church, Chestnut Creek Baptist Church, Maple Springs Baptist Church, Mount Pisgah Methodist Church, Poplar Springs Baptist Church, Samaria Baptist Church, Verbena Cemetery
- County Courthouse Addresses
- Early Marshall County Marriages
- Evans Cemetery, located near Sulligent in Lamar County, Alabama
- Fayette County, Alabama Cemetery Records
- Find-A-Grave by Location - Alabama
- Graves of noteworthy people
- Greene County, Alabama Marriages 1823-1860
- Henry County, Alabama Cemetery Listings
- Index of Graves at Liberty Hill Primitive Baptist Cemetery
- Index to Obituaries Taken from the Southern Democrat, Blount County, Alabama 1915 - 1940
- Interment.net: Alabama Cemeteries
- Inventory of Online Records for Mobile County, Alabama & Nearby
- Lawrence County Marriages
- National Archives - Southeast Region (Alabama records)
- The Obituary Link Page - Alabama Obituary Links
- Old Huntsville Magazine - Cemetery Records of Madison County, Alabama
- Old Huntsville Magazine - Huntsville City Directory 1859-1860
- Old Huntsville Magazine - A Listing of Cemeteries in Madison County, Alabama
- Old Huntsville Magazine - Purchasers of Huntsville Town Lots from Original Owners
- Pickens County, Alabama Marriages 1881-1898
- Pleasant Grove Methodist Cemetery
- Chilton County, Alabama, 1848-1978
- The Political Graveyard - Cemeteries in Alabama
- Preplanning Network - Funeral Home and Cemetery Directory - Alabama
- Shelby County, Alabama Cemetery Census Index
- Sumter County, Alabama Marriages 1833-1850
- Tuscaloosa County, Alabama Marriages 1821-1860
- Tuscaloosa County, Alabama Cemeteries
- Union Baptist Church Inscriptions - Lipscomb, Alabama
- USGenWeb Census Project Alabama
- USGenWeb Tombstone Transcription Project - Alabama
- VitalChek Network - Alabama
- Where to Write for Vital Records - Alabama , from the National Center for Health Statistics (NCHS).
- Your Toolshed for Research, from the Southern Leaves and Branches Site. Records from Conecuh, Covington and Escambia counties.

Summary — Search Local and State Sources

A family researcher's job is to find the place on the ground where an ancestor lived. With that accomplished, the doors open for detailed research in local and state resources.

Local and state genealogical resources provide evidence of people's lives. County courthouse records, and sources located near the place an ancestor lived can be the best evidence that a person lived in a certain place at a certain time. The incidental evidence of a name on a tax list or census, or land record, a burial, or some reference to a person in a court record can lead to the important genealogical evidence needed to compile a family tree.

Search the National Sources

Records at the National Archives

The National Archives has more than one million cubic feet of records that document American history from the time of the First Continental Congress and holds valuable records of the three branches of the federal government. Records with genealogical value are those which refer to a person's name, a date, and an involvement in some activity under the control of the federal government. Records that document censuses, immigration, naturalization, military service, and the settlement of public lands are examples of federal papers that can confirm a person's ancestry, residence, marriage, and many more facts about a person.

There are thousands of records with genealogical value maintained at the National Archives and Records Administration (NARA). It is estimated that over 65,000 rolls of microfilm at the National Archives have genealogical significance. Because of their importance to genealogy, census records are described separately. Perhaps the most important national genealogical source records, census records provide the names, dates of residence, and often much more family information for the general population of the United States, from 1790-1920. The locations, addresses, and Internet web sites for all of the branches of the National Archives were identified in *Step 5 — Search the Census Records!*

The historical records found at the National Archives with the greatest value need to be surveyed for the possibility of gaining genealogical evidence for your ancestors. The www.nara.gov web site is good place to learn what types of records exist with genealogical value. As an example, here are some of the most important ones:

Records of Immigrant Arrivals in America

Customs Passenger Lists. Through the U.S. Customs Service, the federal government has been recording the names of passengers aboard ships arriving in America since 1798, and for many different ports of entry to the United States. Most of these original records still exist at the National Archives and Records Administration (NARA).

Passenger arrivals recorded from 1798 to 1820 are mainly baggage lists or cargo manifests from ships arriving in the United States, but many of these lists also show the names of passengers. For this period, the cargo-passenger lists are very fragmented, since there was no uniform national policy to the handling of the ship manifests until 1819.

An Act of March 2, 1819 required vessels to deliver to the U.S. Customs a manifest (list of names) of all the passengers coming to the United States. An original manifest was prepared on board a ship, sworn to by the master of the vessel, and filed with the collector of customs when the ship arrived at the port. The manifest usually contained the name of the vessel, name of the master, name of port of embarkation, date of arrival, name of port of arrival, and for each passenger, a name, age, sex, occupation, name of country of origin, country of intended settlement, and date and circumstances of death en route, if applicable. The information was recorded for all passengers, including immigrants, tourists, or U.S. citizens returning from abroad.

The surviving U.S. Customs passenger lists from U.S. ports are now stored at the National Archives, and most of them have been microfilmed. Since the lists are arranged by port and date of arrival, finding a person's name in the lists often requires an exact understanding of the time and place of arrival of an ancestor to America. However, many of the lists have been indexed.

Immigration Passenger Lists. An act of 1882 established procedures for immigrants arriving in the United States. The records maintained by federal immigration officials were often called Immigration Passenger Lists or manifests. The lists are part of the records of the Immigration and Naturalization Service (formerly the Bureau of Immigration). The National Archives has microfilm copies of these lists, dated generally 1883-1945, and for all ports of embarkation in the United States.

For the first few years after 1882, the Immigration Passenger Lists were prepared by the various port authorities, following a format of their own choosing. Each list contained at least the following information: name of vessel, name of port, arrival date, and for each passenger, a name, place of birth, age, and sex. In 1893, a standardized format was implemented by the Bureau of Immigration and used thereafter at all U.S. ports of embarkation.

The 1893 form contained the following information: name of master, name of vessel, names of ports of arrival and embarkation, date of arrival, and the following information for each passenger: full name, age; sex; marital status; occupation; nationality; last residence; final destination; whether going to join a relative and if so, the relative's name, address, and relationship to the passenger. In 1903 the form added the race of each passenger, and in 1906, the name and address of the nearest relative in the immigrant's home country was given. Included in the lists were immigrants, tourists, and U.S. citizens returning from abroad.

For some ports, there are separate lists for aliens and for citizens. Lists of citizens show for each passenger, a name, age, sex, and marital status; date and place of birth if born in the United States; date of naturalization and name and location of court if applicable; and a current address for the passenger.

Indexes to Passenger Arrivals. The National Archives has microfilmed indexes to the Customs Passenger Lists and Immigration Passenger Lists, as well as the lists themselves, for the following ports: **Baltimore**, 1820-1952; **Boston**, 1848-1892, 1902-1920; **New Orleans**, 1820-1859, 1853-1899; **New York**, 1820-1846, 1897-1943; and **Philadelphia**, 1800-1948, plus a few isolated lists from various other ports. A request can be made to search these indexed passenger lists. Write to the National Archives to obtain a copy of NATF Form 81 (Order for Copies of Ship Passenger Arrival Records) at General Reference Branch (NNRG), National Archives and Records Administration, 7th and Pennsylvania Ave., N.W., Washington, DC 20408. More about requesting information or obtaining copies of request forms from the National Archives can be found at the NARA Internet web site at www.nara.gov

Some of the above passenger list indexes were reproduced on CD-ROM by Palladium Interactive as part of their Ultimate Family Data Library. Palladium products have now been integrated into Broderbund's Family Tree Maker "Family Archives," a CD-ROM data collection. To see the various titles, visit Broderbund's website at www.familytreemaker.com. Then go to "Family Archives CDs," then "Browse the CD Collection by Record Type," and find a list under "Ship Passenger Lists" the titles of several CD-ROM passenger indexes by port and years of coverage.

New York Arrivals, 1846-1897. The lack of NARA indexes to New York arrivals from 1846 to 1897 — the period in which the largest number of immigrants came to America — has been a real burden for genealogists. The New York arrivals for 1846-1897 are organized in chronological order by the year, month, and name of ship, and there is no complete index. For years, the process of locating an immigrant's name in a passenger list to New York for this period has been one of searching a particular year for a particular ship, and hoping to find a particular name listed on one of the manifests — a daunting endeavor. But the good news is that there are several recent indexing projects that will bring this critical period into better focus.

Some index projects have been undertaken through the sponsorship of a few private parties, such as a company in Colorado, DigArchCo, who has been digitizing and indexing several ship passenger lists and publishing them on CD-ROM. (See their website at www.digarc.com).

But the largest index projects have been those conducted through the Balch Institute for Ethnic Studies at Temple University in Philadelphia. Several names indexes to passenger arrivals in New York and other ports have been done. Currently, in cooperation with the Ellis Island Foundation, the Balch Institute is working to complete name indexes of all New York immigrant arrivals that passed through Ellis Island (1870s through the 1920s).

The Balch Institute's projects have produced some very useful indexes. For example, there are now published name lists from passenger arrivals for the following ethnic groups and time periods:

• Glazier, Ira A. and Tepper, Michael, eds. *The Famine Immigrants: List of the Irish Immigrants Arriving at the Port of New York, 1846-51*, 7 vols. (Baltimore: Genealogical Publishing Co., Inc., 1983-86)

• Glazier, Ira A. and P. William Filby, eds., *Germans to America: Lists of Passengers Arriving at U.S. Ports, 1850 —*. (Wilmington: Scholarly Resources, Inc., 1988-96). Currently available: Vol. 1 (Jan. 1850) — Vol. 59 (Nov. 1890).

• Glazier, Ira A. and P. William Filby, eds., *Italians to America: List of Passengers Arriving at U.S. Ports, 1880 —* . (Wilmington: Scholarly Resources, Inc., 1992-96). Currently available: Vol. 1 (Jan. 1880) — Vol. 9 (June 1896).

• Glazier, Ira A., ed., *Migration from the Russian Empire: List of Passengers arriving at the Port of New York, 1875 —* . (Baltimore: Genealogical Publishing Co., Inc. 1995 —). Currently available: Vol. 1 (Jan. 1875) to Vol. 6 (June 1891).

For more information about the Balch Institute's Ship Manifests, visit their Internet website at www.libertynet.org/balch/static/html/body_ship_manifests.html

Some of the published Balch (book) indexes above are now available as CD-ROM publications. See the Heritage Quest catalog at www.heritagequest.com for titles, prices, and ordering information. Or, go the Genealogical Publishing Co., Inc. website at www.genealogybookshop.com to see the titles published by that company. At GPC's site, do a keyword search for the word "passenger" which will bring up about 40 titles, including several CD-ROM indexes to ship passenger lists.

Naturalization Records

The first naturalization act, passed in 1790, provided that an alien who desired to become a citizen of the United States should apply to "any common law court of record, in any one of the states wherein he shall have resided for the period of one year at least." Under this and later laws, aliens were naturalized in federal, state, county, or municipal courts.

Records of aliens naturalized by way of local or state courts may still be located at the courthouse of that jurisdiction, or may have been removed for safe keeping to a state archives. Records of those aliens naturalized by way of the District Courts of the United States are located today in the District Court covering all or part of a particular state, or the National Archives branch facility covering that state's federal court records.

The process of naturalization involved several steps, for which multiple documents with genealogical information may exist along the way:

Declarations of Intention are documents by which applicants for U.S. citizenship renounced allegiance to foreign sovereignties and declared their intention to become a U.S. citizen. As the first step in the naturalization process, they were often called "First Papers." Early declarations of intention usually show for each applicant, a full name, country of birth or allegiance, date of the application, and a signature. Some will show a date and port of arrival in the United States.

After 1906, a longer and more detailed form was used, including such information as the applicant's name, age, occupation, and personal description; date and place of birth; citizenship; present address and last foreign address; vessel and port of embarkation for the United States; U.S. port and date of arrival in the United States; and date of application and signature.

Naturalization Petitions are documents by which those who had declared their intention to become a U.S. citizen made formal application for citizenship, after meeting the residency requirements. Information on these documents includes a full name, residence, occupation, date and place of birth, citizenship, and personal description of applicant (many 20th century documents include a photograph); date of immigration; port of embarkation and arrival; marital status; names, dates, and places of birth for the applicant's children; date at which U.S. residence commenced; time of residence in state; name changes; and a signature.

Naturalization Depositions are formal statements in support of an applicant's petition by witnesses designated by the applicant. The records indicate the period of the applicant's residence in a certain locale and other information, including witnesses' appraisals of the applicant's character.

Certificates of Naturalization and **Oaths of Allegiance** document the granting of U.S. citizenship to petitioners. The early orders of admission to citizenship are often available only in the minute books of the court where the final naturalization certificate was issued. The minute books are organized in chronological order, but have an index to the names. In some case, all records for one person undergoing the naturalization process have been gathered together in a petition record folder, which usually includes the petition for naturalization, affidavits of the petitioner and witnesses, the oath of allegiance, and the order of the court admitting the petitioner to citizenship.

The Certificate of Naturalization was given to the new citizen but no copy of the certificate was kept by the court that issued it. Only a minute book record or a copy of the court order, and possibly the Oath of Allegiance was recorded and kept at local courthouse. From 1906 forward, copies of all naturalization documents generated at the local courts were sent to the Immigration and Naturalization Service in Washington, DC, where copies of all First Papers, Petitions, Depositions, Oaths of Allegiance, and Certificates of Naturalization can be found today.

As an example of naturalization records initiated at the Federal District Court for the Southern District of Alabama (Mobile), the early records are now at the National Archives and Records Administration — Southeast Region, located in East Point, a suburb of Atlanta, Georgia. Records include petition and record documents, 1906-1929, and declarations of intention, 1855-1929. They are all indexed by the name of the petitioner.

Naturalization Records Since 1906

The Immigration and Naturalization Service (INS) has copies of all naturalization records (certificates, declarations of intentions, and petitions), since September 27, 1906. They are completely indexed. A request for information from a naturalization file must be done on Form G-639. A copy of that form can be downloaded from the INS web site at http://www.ins.usdoj.gov/graphics/formsfee/forms/

Naturalization Information Found in Other Federal Records

Other federal records that provide naturalization information are **passport applications,** among the General Records of the Department of State, Record Group 59, and **homestead applications,** in the Records of the Bureau of Land Management, Record Group 49. If a naturalized citizen applied for a passport before 1906, records of his naturalization are usually in the passport application file. In some cases, a copy of a Certificate of Naturalization can be found in an applicant's file.

Foreign born homestead applicants had to present evidence of citizenship or that they had declared their intention to become a citizenship to qualify for homestead land. As a result, naturalization declarations or certificates are often found in the case files of homestead land entries. (See Essay 1 — Federal Land Records, for more information about homesteads and other land entries).

Naturalization Records Not in the National Archives

To obtain information about naturalization records that are not in the custody of the National Archives, a genealogist should write to the appropriate court official, usually the clerk of the court that issued the certificate of naturalization. If the petitioner were naturalized after September 27, 1906, federal law required that copies of the naturalization documents from any court must be sent to the Immigration and Naturalization Service (INS) (formerly the Bureau of Immigration). Therefore, after 1906, there may be two sets of records, one set at the local courthouse, another at the INS.

Military Pension Records

Military records make up a large part of the National Archives of the United States. Those that relate to military personnel constitute a rich source for genealogical research. They fall into two categories: evidence of military service, and evidence of veteran's benefits. The service, of course, preceded the benefits. But a researcher might begin with the pension files. A veteran's or his widow's application for a pension may provide most of the genealogical information sought: the veteran's age and residence at the date of application, the names of his wife and children, and the dates of marriage and death. A pension file will also provide specific information about the veteran's military service, including the name of his unit and dates of service, and other essential keys to the search for other evidence of his military service. In using the service records, a research must know when and where an ancestor served and whether he was a volunteer, regular Army or Navy, or whether he was an enlisted man or an officer. These distinctions are less important for searches in the pension applications.

The National Archives has pension applications and records of pension payments for veterans, their widows, and other heirs. They are based on all military service in the armed forces of the United States between 1775 and 1916, with the exception of military service for the Confederate States of America, 1861-65.

Pension files at the National Archives number in the millions. They are divided by the major series: Revolutionary War, Old Wars, War of 1812, Indian Wars, Mexican War, Civil War, and later service. The records in each series are arranged alphabetically by the name of the veteran, except those in the Civil War series and later, which are arranged numerically by application, certificate, or file number. All series of pension applications have alphabetical name indexes.

Military Service Records

Volunteer Service Records. If your ancestor served as a volunteer in the military before World War I, the National Archives almost certainly has a record of that service. With excellent indexes to these records available, copies of papers relating to a soldier's military service are easy to obtain. Military service records from as early as 1775 exist for individuals who served as volunteers (non-regular, militia, or draftees) and for those serving Regular Army, Navy, or Marine Corps units. Over the years, mostly in the latter half of the 19th century, the American military service records of volunteer soldiers were gathered together and abstracted onto cards from muster and pay rolls, rank rolls, returns, hospital records, prison records, accounts for subsistence, and other records. The card abstracts for each individual soldier were placed into a jacket-envelope bearing the soldier's name, rank, and military unit. The jacket-envelopes, each containing one or more abstracts and, in some cases, original documents relating specifically to one soldier, are called the Compiled Military Service Records.

Compiled Military Service Records cover a period of service for volunteers who served during the Revolutionary War, 1775-83; the post-Revolutionary War period, 1784-1811; the War of 1812, 1812-15; Indian Wars, 1816-60; the Mexican War, 1846-48; the Civil War, 1861-65; and the Spanish-American War and the Philippine Insurrection, 1898-1903.

The records are arranged by war or period of service, thereafter by state or other designation, then by the military unit, and finally, by the name of the soldier. There are General Indexes containing the names of all soldiers. In addition, soldiers serving with a unit bearing a state name as part of its official designation, i.e., the 1st Virginia Militia, were also indexed in State Indexes, except for records of the Mexican War and the Philippine Insurrection. Each index card contains the soldier's name, rank, and military unit. Records of the volunteers are better organized and more easily accessible because after the Civil War, the War Department undertook extensive projects to organize, consolidate, and index the service records for volunteer soldiers and their widows applying for a pension.

Regular Army Service Records. From the beginning of this country, the Adjutant General of the United States has had the job of maintaining records for the activities of the Regular Army. In addition to records concerning activities of the military, all correspondence between the War Department and the field, and other record keeping, many of the Adjutant General's records were maintained for individual officers and enlisted men.

Unlike the Compiled Service Records for volunteer soldiers, service records of the soldiers of the Regular Army remain in the various record groups as they were first organized. The types of records maintained since 1775 include the following, each of which has significant genealogical information:

Records Relating to Officers and Enlisted Men. The central files of the Adjutant General's Office have a large number of records about matters relating to individual servicemen. Letters received or sent by the Adjutant General to and from various war departments, bureaus, and military units concerning officers and enlisted men have been indexed.

Muster Rolls. These lists of troops are useful for identifying individual officers and enlisted men. They may include dates of enlistment, period of enlistment, disposition of medical status, and other details. They are organized by the military units for which a servicemen served.

Carded Medical Records. These records contain information about regular army personnel admitted to hospitals for treatment.

Navy and Marine Service Records. Records Relating to Service in the U.S. Navy and U.S. Marine Corp (Record Groups 24, 125, and 127) includes Indexes to Rendezvous Reports, Navy Enlistments through 1884; and indexes to World War I and later records.

World War I Draft Registrations

The World War I draft registrations of men took place between June 5, 1917 and September 12, 1918. During that period, over 24 million men were registered for the draft. Those men registered for the draft had to be citizens of the United States, or had declared their intention to become a citizen. Each registrant's vital statistics was recorded on a card, including name, sex, race, date of birth, place of birth, marital status, and a name of a parent, spouse, or relative. The original registration cards are stored today at the southeast region of the National Archives located at East Point, Georgia. The registrations were all microfilmed by the Family History Library of Salt Lake City. A good description of the WWI draft registrations and what it takes for a search can be found on the Internet at the online Genealogy Bulletin, a weekly newsletter for genealogists. Use the following address:
www.genealogybulletin.com/archives/HTML/current18.html

Part II
Essays For Genealogical Success

Five Essays:

Federal Land Records

This essay first appeared as an article by William Dollarhide, "Federal Land Records" in the *Genealogy Bulletin*, No. 12 (Oct-Nov-Dec 1991); and also appeared in *Heritage Quest* magazine with some revisions as "Federal Land Records: Send Me the Case Files" in issue No. 81 (May-June 1999).

Land Records First

Genealogists may be missing one of the most exciting sources of family information ever. Did you know that you may have a very good chance of locating a file folder with genealogical information about your ancestor, a file folder with perhaps dozens of sheets of papers in it, all specific to that person? That file folder may have breakthrough genealogical information in it, but most genealogists do not know where that file folder is located, nor do they know how to get copies from it. The "very good chance" comes from the fact that ninety percent of all adult white males in America have owned land. In the early days of this country, most people bought their land from the federal government. If so, there is a file folder regarding that land sale, and in that file folder may be some hidden treasures. Would you like to know more about where that file folder is located?

If I have gotten your attention, let's start our discovery of that file folder by talking about America's first president, George Washington. You remember him. George began his working life in Virginia as an apprentice surveyor. He learned well the skills of surveying land and was a qualified professional surveyor while still a teenager. As a surveyor, Washington understood the significance of transportation as it related to the lay of the land and was involved in several surveys for the construction of roads and canals in colonial America. As President, Washington lent his surveying expertise to several proposals for the development of the vast western expanse of the United States. As part of his vision for America, Washington once drew up a plan for a national transportation network, a highlight of which was a major water canal and river route from the Atlantic coast to the Mississippi River, a plan engineers today would call somewhat ambitious, but technically feasible. Many years later, Washington's visionary water route plan was actually attempted when the Chesapeake-Ohio Canal was begun in the 1820s. The canal was never completed all the way, but the same route it was to follow became the route of the Baltimore & Ohio Railroad in the 1840s. Washington may not have seen the future of steamships, railroads, or superhighways, but he knew a transportation link between the Atlantic states and the Mississippi River was going to be a necessary and vital part of America's future.

Washington also supported the concept of land ownership by Americans as the means of opening the western regions of the new country to settlement. Before he became President, he supported the Ordinance of 1787, drawn up by the Continental Congress. This was the first law relating to land expansion, the creation of new territories, and the provision for the sale of public land directly by the federal government to private individuals. During his eight years as President, Washington signed into law several bills relating to public land sales and other land-related issues. He was a strong proponent of western expansion and voiced his support for the construction of roads and canals and, most of all, the availability of cheap land to all Americans.

America's third president, Thomas Jefferson, also had a vision for America. He was an avid expansionist who enthusiastically supported the idea of the United States acquiring land from the Atlantic to the Pacific. It was during Jefferson's presidency in 1803 that the Louisiana Purchase doubled the size of the United States. Jefferson had long advocated that the U.S. acquire New Orleans to give the country guaranteed access to the Mississippi River. When he sent James Madison and Robert Livingston to Paris to negotiate the purchase of New Orleans from Napoleon, he did not expect to be offered all of Louisiana. But when Napoleon offered to sell the entire region, essentially the massive area of drainage for the Mississippi and Missouri Rivers, the surprised and delighted American negotiators quickly accepted the offer. When Jefferson heard that his emissaries had agreed to the Louisiana Purchase, he wholeheartedly supported the idea and it was through his influence with congress that the Louisiana Purchase was approved.

The timing of history could not have been better for the fledgling United States. Except for New Orleans, Louisiana had been a Spanish possession for decades until Napoleon acquired that tract of land as spoils of war after his defeat of Spain in battle. Napoleon knew he could not fight a war in

Europe and maintain any real presence in Louisiana, so he sold it to raise money for his upcoming trip to Moscow. We all know what happened to Napoleon in Russia, so as a footnote to history, Napoleon's greed and failed quest to conquer the world contributed greatly to America's growth and prosperity. There was only a two-year window in which America could have realistically acquired Louisiana from France — the Spanish would have had nothing to do with such a sale to the U.S.

The Louisiana Purchase fit in perfectly with Jefferson's vision for America. He felt that by acquiring the vast region of Louisiana, that the American people could best satisfy their *pursuit of happiness*, a phrase Jefferson had authored in the Declaration of Independence. What Jefferson really wanted was for every male citizen to own a piece of land. By doubling the size of the U.S., there would be unlimited land available, and the needs of a family could be answered. A family with land could support themselves by growing crops, raising animals, and taking care of the basic necessities of life. In Jefferson's view, a successful farmer was one who not only supported his family but could produce a surplus of crops, produce, or livestock that could be taken to local markets for barter or sale.

The Jeffersonian concept was appropriate for an agrarian society, and the ideas were proposed several decades before the advent of the Industrial Revolution. From the very beginning of American society to the mid 1850s, the visions of Washington and Jefferson were realized, and over 90 percent of the inhabitants of the United States were engaged in agriculture. It was not until the 1850s that the Industrial Revolution caused people to move from their farms and head for the cities to live. Manufacturing began to flourish, and people began to move away from their farms for wages in the manufacturing plants in the cities.

Jefferson also had a plan for the creation of new states west of the Appalachian Mountains. He even drew up a map showing the size, arrangement, and names of the new states. Although his specific plan was never adopted, it set the stage for the way Congress was to divide up the public domain into new territories for years to come.

The huge expansion of the United States from 1787 to the mid 1850s and the social and civil consequences of that expansion can be directly tied to the sale of public land to individuals. The reality of land ownership for nearly every American became the single most important factor in explaining why millions of Americans were willing to leave homes in the East and take up new homes in the wilderness of the West. The American government's policy during this period has been called one of "Manifest Destiny" — the so-called God-given right of the U.S. to take possession of the continent by any means at its disposal. During this period, all American political issues were dominated with the ways and means of furthering the American expansion, Indian matters, and public land sales. The issues of preemption (squatters rights), Indian land rights, military land grants, cash and credit land sales, and private land claims overshadowed all other issues except war. Presidents, senators, and congressmen were elected to office based on their stated positions on preemption, public land sales, and related land matters. It was political suicide for a candidate for public office to be opposed to continued land sales by the federal government. And, for America's first 100 years, no other subject in Congress has the volume of legislative action, proposed or enacted, that is not related to a land issue of some kind.

Coinciding with the national issues were similar issues raging at the local level of government. During the period 1790-1850, most of the civil court cases in county court proceedings were related to land disputes. In addition, the predominate subject of county probate courts was an attempt to determine the rightful heirs to a deceased person's land. As a result, there are more extant records relating to land sales, land ownership, land disputes, and land records in general during this period than virtually any other type of written record.

The fact that land ownership has always been so important in America gives genealogists perhaps the most important set of records for identifying their ancestors. It is estimated that up to 1860, over ninety percent of all white adult males in America owned land. That figure means that a researcher who uses land records has a ninety percent chance of finding an ancestor. There is no other set of records with such a high percentage of success in locating the name of a person in historical records.

Yet, land records are not commonly used by genealogists with any great passion. This is because, at first look, land records tend to be unexciting documents with little genealogical value. Many genealogists see land records as secondary resources, because they seem to give little genealogical evidence other than a person's name.

But, in fact, land records apply to most adult white males who ever lived in this country from its very beginnings in the 1600s to the present. They are the most complete records, go back further in time, and are the records with the least amount of destruction compared to any other type of record available to genealogists in their family research. Land records not only confirm the place where an ancestor lived; they may give exact genealogical evidence of his age, place of birth, spouse, children, and other facts. Which of these genealogical clues can be gleaned from land records depends on the time period, the area of the country, and the type of land transaction involved.

This essay will attempt to explain the genealogical importance of public land records, by reviewing the land records generated over the years, the agency that created the records, the location of these records today, and how to access them. Mainly, we hope to demonstrate that the value of land records is great, that land records should not be the *last thing* a genealogist uses in identifying their ancestors, but perhaps the *first thing* a genealogist uses. Moreover, land records for genealogical purposes may provide the most important clue a genealogist will ever find that confirms where and when a person lived in America. Therefore, an understanding of how land sales in America were processed and recorded is important. A genealogist needs to know where the old land sales were first recorded and where the same land records are today. He or she also needs to know whether the records are held by the states or the federal government. To do this, a little more American history may be in order.

Public Land — a Short History

A major concern for the Continental Congress of 1785 was how to finance the operations of the new federal government. Since the first union of 1776, the thirteen states had subsidized the Congress, the Continental Army, and all aspects of fighting a war with Britain. After the war, responsibility for such things as customs and duties on commerce with other countries was the first of many powers given up by the thirteen original states. But, for the new proposed federal government to have an adequate and continuing source of revenue, it was necessary for the original states to cede (give up claim to) western lands they each claimed as their own. It was determined that the new federal government was to earn its own revenue by selling land to people. This determination was a key element in the ratification of the Constitution, by reaffirming the ordinances passed by the Second Continental Congress. It was not easy to ask a land-rich state such as Georgia to give up over half of its land without a fight. In fact, Georgia was the last of the thirteen states to cede western lands to the U.S. government. These lands later became the states of Alabama and Mississippi.

By 1786, the states of Connecticut, Massachusetts, and Virginia all ceded their western lands north and west of the Ohio River to the federal government. This land transfer was confirmed by each state's ratification of the Constitution by 1789. All three states had claimed the same area, based on their royal charters dating back to the 1600s. By ceding their western lands, the way was clear for the federal government to create a new governmental entity, called the Territory Northwest of the Ohio River. Ownership of this new area of land fell into the hands of the federal government and was commonly referred to as the "public domain." Congress had passed the Ordinance of 1787 which set down the principles of land sales in the public domain, as well as the provisions for the creation of new territories. One provision was that any new land added to the United States, such as the Louisiana Purchase, would be added to the Public Domain. Essentially, the original states could never get any larger since any new land added to the United States would become part of the Public Domain.

However, the thirteen states, by ceding their western lands, retained ownership of the land left within their boundaries after any cessions to the federal government. As it turns out, five new states carved from the bounds of the original thirteen states also retained ownership of their lands. And, two states joined the Union under extraordinary conditions and retained ownership by special acts of Congress: Texas and Hawaii. So, the "state-land" states, those which retained ownership of their lands, are the original thirteen states, plus Vermont, Kentucky, Tennessee, Maine, West Virginia, Texas, and Hawaii, for a total of twenty states. All of the other states, thirty in all, are called "public-land" states. The lands in these public land areas (or public domain) were all originally owned by the federal government.

Of course, much of the public domain has been sold off; but a large quantity still lies in the hands of the federal government, much to the consternation of the western states. Today the "sagebrush rebellion" is being fought by the western states to take control of their lands. To date, the federal government has rarely been a willing participant in turning federal land over to the states. The Taylor Grazing Act of 1934 essentially ended land grants to individuals in this country, with a few exceptions in the western states and some homesteads still going on in Alaska. The U.S. government is by far the largest land owner in America due its historical position as the dispensing agent for all public land.

To genealogists, a distinction between state-land states and public-land states is important. If a person's land was in one of the state-land states, the land records are now located in one of the twenty different state land offices, while land records for the thirty public-land states are all maintained by the federal government. This essay is about the thirty public land states.

The huge interior region of the Louisiana Purchase acquired from France and added to the United States in 1803 was immediately divided into two new territories: Louisiana Territory (later named Missouri Territory) and Orleans Territory (which is nearly the same today as the state of Louisiana). Land purchases and annexations continued for another 50 years with the addition of Florida, the Oregon Country, and the annexation of most of Colorado, all of Utah, New Mexico, and Arizona. In the year 1846 alone, the land area of the United States increased in size similar to the Louisiana Purchase. And, in 1850, California was added to the Union as a state without ever having the status of a territory. In 1850, the boundaries of the United States stretched from sea to sea, fulfilling the visions of George Washington and Thomas Jefferson.

First Land Sales in the Northwest Territory

The first step in creating the public domain came when the Continental Congress passed the Land Ordinance of 1785 and took control of most of the region northwest of the Ohio River as federal land. In that same year, a former Revolutionary War General and Boston businessman had a great idea. He was Rufus Putnam. He knew that the new United States was filled with thousands of former revolutionary soldiers, all of whom had been paid a suit of clothes and promise of land "out west somewhere" in the form of a certificate called a Bounty-land Warrant. These certificates had a set value of $1.25 per acre of land, but a soldier would have to travel to the great western wilderness and claim his parcel of land. The certificates could be legally assigned (sold), and the buyer of the certificate would then gain the claim to wilderness land "out west somewhere."

So, Rufus Putnam devised a plan to buy certificates from former Revolutionary Soldiers and for a fraction of their face value. He then figured out a way to combine these certificates for obtaining large tracts of land in the western wilderness. Rufus was to become a land speculator, using the time-honored rule of "buy low sell high." First, he had to convince about ten of his business friends in Boston to invest in his plan. A company was formed called the "New Ohio Company." By 1787, the company was able to obtain warrants representing millions of acres of land "out west somewhere" purchased from soldiers.

The New Ohio Company did not have trouble buying these certificates from the former soldiers. Everyone knew that going out west was dangerous. There were hostile Indians out there who had supported the British during the war and disliked Americans. There were no troops to protect the settlers, and there were no decent roads to get there. So, when someone offered to buy your land warrant, you jumped at the chance to sell it. It is estimated that over ninety percent of all Revolutionary War Land Warrants were sold in this way.

The New Ohio Company agents set up shop in New York City. Their first "shop" was a soap box on a street corner where a hawker would call out to passers-by that he was buying land warrants. That soap box was on Wall Street. The practice of buying and selling land warrants was the beginning of the New York Stock Exchange.

Rufus Putnam's agents at the U.S. Capital in New York City were well connected. Rufus managed to convince legislators drawing up the Ordinance of 1787, the act which established the Territory Northwest of the Ohio River, to include a huge land grant for the New Ohio Company. Based on his assignments of bounty-land warrants, plus purchases on credit, his company's land grant was drawn on a map (north of the Ohio River, including all of present-day Washington County, Ohio) and exempted from the lands to be sold by the federal government. He also managed to gain much more land by agreeing to honor any soldier's bounty-land warrants in the area granted to the company. All in all, Rufus and his associates managed to purchase seven million acres of land in the Northwest Territory for an average price of eight cents per acre. Some of the land was paid for using bounty-land warrants, and a small down payment was made for the rest. Rufus Putnam began his land office in Marietta, a town he founded on the Ohio River.

Rufus said he was willing to manage his company's large tract of land, sell to private buyers, and act as an agent for the federal government. Congress saw nothing wrong with this plan and voted for it, mainly because Congress had not yet developed a method of selling land itself. Essentially, the New Ohio Company became a land broker for the federal government and was selling land in the new Northwest Territory well before the federal government began selling land there. Putnam told Congress he would pay for the land as soon as he sold it. What a deal!

Following Rufus Putnam's lead, Judge John Cleves Symmes, a former senator from New Jersey, decided to get into the land business in the Ohio country as well. The "Symmes Purchase" (or "Miami Purchase") began as a one-million acre tract of land between the Miami and Little Miami Rivers and included Cincinnati and what is now Hamilton County, Ohio. Symmes set up his land office in Cincinnati and began offering land to settlers.

Putnam, Symmes, and a few other land brokers dominated land sales in the Northwest Territory for the first ten years of its existence. The United States Government, through the Treasury Department, had established its first land office in New York City in 1787, but most land sales in the new territory were being conducted by land brokers. The first direct government sales began in 1797 for an area called the "seven ranges," bordering Pennsylvania. The first field office to make land sales within the Northwest Territory was established in Steubenville in 1800.

Public Land Records — the Process

Prior to the 20th century, our American ancestors did not pay income tax. The major source of revenue for the federal government was from sale of public lands. Of course, by 1920, virtually all of the good farmland in America had been sold, and Uncle Sam had to pick our pockets for operating cash.

My great-great-grandfather, Jesse Dollarhide, died in 1840 without the benefit of ever knowing what "IRS" stood for. In fact, Jesse's only direct contact with the U.S. Government, aside from voting in national elections, was in 1838, when he purchased 160 acres from the federal government. He bought a quarter section of prime farmland in Tippecanoe County, Indiana. Jesse bought the land at a Government Land Office (GLO) conveniently located in Crawfordsville, Indiana, about 30 miles south of where the land was located. Jesse paid for the 160 acres all at once with a cash payment of $320.00. He paid this amount, even though he could have purchased the land with a down-payment of ten percent of the purchase price, or $32.00. He would have then had five years to pay off the balance. For such credit land sales, the local GLO kept records of payments made by the buyer. If, during the course of the five-year payment period, a buyer could not continue the payments, or died, a record of the incomplete land transaction was made and can still be found in the papers maintained by the local GLO.

The steps in purchasing land in the Crawfordsville GLO in 1838 was the same in all 362 Government Land Offices that have ever existed, beginning with the first GLO established in Steubenville, Ohio in 1800, and the last created in New Castle, Wyoming in 1920. First, a record of the land transaction was recorded in a "plat book," which was a bound volume of maps. Each map page showed an outline of one federal township, a 36 square mile area, six miles across and six miles deep.

A federal township is divided into 36 equal sections, each section being one mile square. (One square mile is 640 acres of land.) Jesse Dollarhide's name and an outline drawing of the 160 acres (a quarter section) he had purchased was sketched onto a map sheet in the plat book. Next, Jesse's name was recorded in a "tract book," which was a tabulated journal showing his name, file number, date of purchase, type of sale, and a description of the property being purchased. The tract book agreed with the plat book, with one page for each federal township. A land buyer was referred to as an "entryman." All of the entrymen purchasing land within one federal township were listed in both the tract book and the plat book.

The File Folder

In addition to the plat book and tract book, another set of documents were maintained at the Crawfordsville land office, such as any correspondence relating to the land sale, copies of receipts, petitions, applications, and any other papers relating to Jesse's land purchase. These papers were all loosely filed together in a file folder. Today they are called "land entry case files" — and these are the public land records with the most genealogical information, and form the basis for this essay.

Each land transaction was given a case number. The case number also appeared on the plat book, usually written under the name of the entryman and entered into the tract book. A plat book entry, a tract book entry, and other papers (in a file folder) were created for every land transaction, whether or not the land sale was ever completed. About ten percent of all land transactions were never consummated, yet the case files for all incomplete land transaction still exist. Evidence of such an incomplete land transaction was found for Jesse's son, John Dollarhide, who entered a land claim in 1851 but never completed it. Instead, John left Indiana for Illinois but a record of his first petition for a land purchase in Indiana still exists, including a case file folder with several papers relating to his petition for a land purchase.

Two federal clerks worked at the Crawfordsville GLO. One clerk held the title of Receiver and collected all monies for cash sales of land. The other clerk was called a Recorder and was the keeper of the plat books and tract books. Both books were large preprinted bound volumes. When all of the pages of a tract book or plat book were filled, the Recorder was asked to make a handwritten copy of the full book and then send the copy to the Surveyor General's office in Washington, DC. So, there were actually two original copies of the plat and tract books. The "first original" is the one that sat on the GLO counter every day and weathered coffee spills, cigar burns, and daily handling. The "second original" was prepared by the Recorder to be mailed to Washington, and, presumably, the copy that would be read by his boss, the Surveyor General of the United States. Not surprising, the second original is cleaner and easier to read than the first original but may contain transcription errors. The second originals, the best copies, are now located in one of two offices near Washington, DC.

For the Crawfordsville, Indiana, GLO and all other land offices, the records were transferred to the Surveyor General of the United States, including all of the case file folders identified by the case file number. Accessing these file folders is a step every genealogist should take. The genealogical information in the file folders may reveal previously unknown treasures to a researcher.

In the Eastern States Branch of the Bureau of Land Management (BLM) located at Springfield, Virginia, the original records of Jesse Dollarhide's entry of land reside in the form of a plat book and tract book transferred from the Crawfordsville GLO. In addition, the document which is the proof of ownership can be found, called a *patent*. The patent is a certificate which identifies the land, confirms the details of the land transfer, date, place, and acts as the written proof of ownership. Until well into the 1840s, all patents issued by the U.S. Government were signed personally by the sitting President of the United States. All patents were numbered and filed in numerical sequence. Jesse Dollarhide received a patent. A copy of his patent was retained by the Surveyor General's office in Washington, DC.

Historically, a patent is the same as a deed, and its use in British history dates back to the time of William the Conqueror. The patent was the device used to transfer ownership of land from a sovereign to an individual. The term has been used in America since its very beginnings but applies to the original transfer of land from a king, governor, colony, state, or since 1787, the United States Government.

The Springfield, Virginia, BLM office now has the original patents, plat books, and tract books for the Crawfordsville Land Office as well as all other land offices for 13 eastern states: Alabama, Arkansas, Florida, Illinois, Indiana, Iowa, Louisiana, Michigan, Minnesota, Mississippi, Missouri, Ohio, and Wisconsin. Not far away, at the National Archives I branch in Washington, D.C., the file folder containing all of the paperwork relating to Jesse's land purchase can be found. The case files for all land offices in all thirty public-land states are now located at the National Archives, as well as all plat and tract books for 17 western states: Alaska, Arizona, California, Colorado, Idaho, Kansas, Montana, Nebraska, Nevada, New Mexico, North Dakota, Oklahoma, Oregon, South Dakota, Utah, Washington, and Wyoming. An eastern state, by BLM's definition, is any state east of or touching the Mississippi River (on either side of it).

The land entry files (the file folders) are organized at the National Archives today in the same arrangement they were first created; that is, they are filed first by the state, then by the land office, and within each land office group, numerically by a case file number. The apparent problem is that before a researcher can gain access to the file folder, he must know the state, land office, and the case file number. (But don't give up yet. There is more to come, including complete instructions on how to get copies from that elusive file folder!)

Jesse Dollarhide's land purchase was an "original entry of land." In other words, Jesse was the first buyer/owner of a certain parcel of land purchased from the United States Government. But there is no known record of that original sale in the courthouse located in Tippecanoe County, Indiana, the county in which the land was situated. Although some counties maintained records of original entries of land within their county bounds, they were not required to do so. If a county recorded federal land sales, they may be found in a record book in the courthouse entitled, "Original Entries of Land." In many cases, however, a researcher will not find a county reference to a federal land sale until after the same property is sold. Any subsequent sales of land are recorded in the form of a deed at the county courthouse wherein the land was located. This is true for all thirty public-land states. So, the keeper of the original records of Jesse's land sale was the federal government. Fortunately, the federal government still has the land records for Jesse Dollarhide's land transaction.

For genealogists, public land records are tremendous resources; and the records are 100% complete. Even the land records destroyed in Washington, DC, during the War of 1812 were not unique and were replaced after the war with duplicate records taken from the various field offices of the Government Land Office. For the 1.5 billion acres of public land sold since 1785, the federal government holds extant land records for virtually every land sale, some 7.5 million land transactions all together.

When Jesse died intestate in 1840, his estate was settled in the probate court of Tippecanoe County. Numerous papers make reference to his land as the "northwest 1/4 section, section 4, township 24 north, range 4 west." Subsequent deeds recorded in Tippecanoe County show later owners of the same land. But to find any paperwork (the file folder) relating to the original sale, it was necessary to learn how one goes about getting such records from the source — the federal government.

Another ancestor, Noah McNemar, left Louisa County, Iowa, in 1850 to seek his fortune in the gold fields of California. He did fairly well; and in 1852, he traveled up to Washington County, Oregon. Soon after his move to Oregon, Noah remarried and took advantage of new way to acquire free land in Oregon called a Donation Land Claim (DLC) (a forerunner of the Homestead Act). A single man could get 320 acres, while a married man could get 640 acres under the provisions of the Donation Land Claim Act. As a married man, Noah entered his land claim for 640 acres at a Government Land Office located at Oregon City, Oregon Territory, in 1853. The papers relating to Noah's land transaction recorded his exact date of birth, that he was a native of Ohio, the name of his new wife; and the exact date and place of their marriage. Those original papers showing genealogical relationships, dates, places, signatures, etc. were discovered at a federal repository, not at a county or state office. In the land entry files in the National Archives (the *file folder*) for Noah McNemar's land transaction is the original marriage certificate for his marriage to Nancy Kurtz in 1853 which is what Noah took to the GLO as proof of his marriage. Clearly, Noah believed that sacrificing the only copy of his marriage certificate was a small price to pay for getting 640 free acres of land from Uncle Sam. (In fact, it is rumored that the only reason that Noah, age 48, married Nancy Kurtz, age 18, was to get double the number of acres for the Donation Land Claim. But, then again, he and Nancy produced six children over the next few years; so it must have been more than a marriage of convenience).

Noah was born in Ohio. But if he had not been a U.S. citizen, he would have had to prove his citizenship, or his intention to become a citizen. This provision was also true for Homestead Entries (1862 and after), making these types of land records very valuable to genealogists, particularly for immigrants who applied for Homestead land. In proving a marriage or evidence of citizenship, an applicant often included a copy of his marriage certificate, or a page torn out of a family Bible, or a copy of his *Intention to become a Citizen of the United States* papers. If an applicant included these types of documents with his petition for land, he never got them back — they are still located in a file folder, now located at the National Archives!

Another example of public land records was for my grandfather, John Conrad Dollarhide. John left his home in Ft. Jones, California, in early 1905 and traveled to southeast Washington. At the Government Land Office in Walla Walla, he filed a Homestead Claim for 160 acres of land located near the town of Dayton, Washington. After building a makeshift cabin, he returned to Ft. Jones, and gathered up his family, and moved from northern California to southeast Washington. My father, Albert Raymond Dollarhide, was responsible for a delay in the journey because he chose that trip to be born. Albert was born in Oakland, Oregon, on April 19, 1905, while the family was en route to their new home. After a few days at the doctor's home in Oakland, the family continued on their trip with the new infant and finally arrived at their new homestead a few miles south of Dayton, Columbia County, Washington. In researching records of Columbia County, I came across a wonderful old county atlas, organized by each township and showing the names of land owners. The atlas was printed in 1912; and, sure enough, a parcel of 160 acres was shown with the name "J.C. Dollarhide, H.E. #19674" written within the space for his property. "H.E." stands for "Homestead Entry," and the number indicated the file number for the land entry. That 1912 atlas gave me the exact case file number for John Dollarhide's land claim! With a only a little more effort, I was able to acquire copies of the entire case file (the file folder) for John Dollarhide's homestead claim, located at the National Archives.

The land entry papers in John C. Dollarhide's homestead file folder were full of genealogy. Most were dated 1910, five years after the homestead claim was first entered. The papers listed the name of John's wife as Addie and named all of their nine children plus their ages in 1910. The papers even gave me the names of neighbors who had signed affidavits attesting to the fact that John Dollarhide had indeed lived on the land for five years, that he had raised crops, and that he had built a house on the property — all requirements for proving a five-year homestead claim.

The land records obtained from the National Archives relating to Jesse Dollarhide's Indiana land purchase in 1838, the Oregon Donation Land Claim of Noah McNemar in 1853, and John Dollarhide's homestead in 1905 have all contributed greatly to my understanding of the lives of these ancestors. These examples are not rare occurrences. Any genealogist can repeat my experience in locating land records for their ancestors and will have a very good chance of success. It all depends on locating an elusive file folder in Washington, DC.

It should be pointed out, however, that the information one will find in the land entry papers (the file folder) will vary from case to case. Generally, the genealogical information increases with later land claims. The earliest records may only reveal a few items such as a receipt or a statement of transmittal. But, over the years, the public land laws were liberalized to include donations and homesteads. These types of land transactions required more paperwork. The records that can be found in the file folders increases in proportion to the increased complexity of the provisions of the land acts starting in 1785. For example, the Donation Land Claim Act applied to Florida and Oregon Territory, began in 1848; and the paperwork was much greater than before. In 1848, Oregon Territory included the present-day area of Oregon, Washington, Idaho, and the parts of Montana and Wyoming west of the continental divide. In 1862, the Homestead Act was passed and applied to land grants in all thirty of the public-land states. Therefore, the amount of genealogical information that one can find in the case file folders will be greater for the later time period of the Donation Land Claims and Homestead Claims.

Accessing the File Folder

A genealogist needs to know that for every land transaction in the public domain, there is a file folder with papers relating to that land transaction. That file folder is where the likelihood of genealogical information will be found. The plat books and tract books should only be considered tools for locating the name of the Government Land Office and the case file number. That file folder today is located in the National Archives I branch in Washington, DC. All the folders are organized by state, then by the local Government Land Office that originated the records. The file folder with all the genealogical goodies is identified with a case file number. It is time to find out how to access that elusive file folder.

All requests for copies of Land Entry Files must be done on a **NATF Form 84.** Therefore, the first step in getting copies is to first get a copy of that form. Once you have obtained a copy of the form, a request can be made. There are several questions that must be answered before the land entry files can be accessed

Here are five test questions to determine the exact steps in accessing the case files relating to any land transaction in the public-land states. At each test question, if you answer "yes" to the question, the steps to obtain copies of the case files will be given. If you answer "no" to any test question, go on to the next test.

Test Question #1:

Was the land entry after 1 January 1908?

If you answered "no" to this question, go to Test Question #2.

If you can answer this question with a "yes", you are in luck. There is a complete name index to the case files for all public land states from 1908 forward, giving the case file number and land office. Write a letter requesting a copy of NATF form 84 from:

> Old Military & Civil — Land Team
> National Archives and Records Administration
> Washington, DC 20408

The minimum information you need to provide is the following:

- the name of the person who obtained land from the federal government
- the state where the land was obtained
- a request for a price quote to make copies of the case files

Test Question #2:

Was the land entry before 1 January 1908… AND, the land entry was in one of these seven indexed states?

> Alabama, Alaska, Arizona, Florida, Louisiana, Nevada, or Utah

If you answered "no" to this question, go to Test Question #3.

If you can answer "yes" to this question, you are in luck. There are complete name indexes to the case files for the seven states listed above. These card indexes were prepared by the WPA in the late 1930s. Each card gives the name of a person who obtained land from the federal government in these seven states only, plus the case file number, and other information.

Write a letter requesting a copy NATF form 84 from:

> Old Military & Civil — Land Team
> National Archives and Records Administration
> Washington, DC 20408

> or, visit the National Archives website at www.nara.gov.

The minimum information you will need to provide on the form is the following:

- the name of the person who obtained land from the federal government
- the state where the land was obtained
- a request for a price quote to make copies of the case files

Test Question #3

Was the land entry before 1 January 1908... AND, the land entry was in one of these thirteen unindexed western States?

California, Colorado, Idaho, Kansas, Montana, Nebraska, New Mexico, North Dakota, Oklahoma, Oregon, South Dakota, Washington, or Wyoming

If you answered "no" to this question, go to Test Question #4.

If you can answer this question with a "yes," write a letter requesting a copy of NATF form 84 from:

> Old Military & Civil — Land Team
> National Archives and Records Administration
> Washington, DC 20408

The minimum information you will need to provide on the form is the following:

- the name of the person who obtained land from the federal government
- the state wherein the land was located
- the exact legal description of the property. An exact legal description MUST be provided, such as: "the northwest 1/4 section, township 24 north, range 4 east, 2nd principal meridian." The National Archives staff will use the property description to locate the correct Government Land Office where the land transaction took place. Once in the correct land office records, they will find the name of the person listed as an entryman in either the plat book or tract book created by that land office. This will lead them to the case file number so they can pull the case files relating to that land transaction. If you do not know the property description, do one of the following:

1. Get the property description from a deed in a courthouse. When the person's land was sold, a property description was recorded on the deed. The property description may be found in the grantee/grantor index to deeds in the courthouse, without having to read the deed itself.

2. Find the property description on a plat map or land ownership atlas where the names of property owners are listed on a map for one federal township. From the map, a property description can be deduced. One page in the atlas is usually one federal township, such as "Township 24 North, Range 4 East."

3. If you have a copy of a patent for the property in question, the file number and land office is shown on the patent. If you have homestead papers, deeds, or any other reference to the land, look for the legal description which should be included in the papers.

Test Question #4

Was the land entry before 1 January 1908 ... AND, the land entry was in one of these nine indexed eastern states?

Arkansas, Indiana, Illinois, Michigan, Minnesota, Mississippi, Missouri, Ohio, or Wisconsin

If you answered "no" to this question, go to Test Question #5.

If you can answer this question with a "yes," write a letter to:

Bureau of Land Management
Eastern States Branch
7450 Boston Blvd.
Springfield, VA 22153.

No form is required. Your letter should provide the following information:

1. The name of the person obtaining land from the federal government
2. The state in which the land was located
3. A request for a copy of the PATENT issued to the person.

NOTE: Since 1989, the Eastern States Branch of the Bureau of Land Management has been indexing the names of patentees for all of the thirteen eastern public-land states. The project is called the GLO Automated Records Project. As of December 1997, the BLM has completed the work to index twelve of the thirteen states under their jurisdiction. Only nine indexed states are shown above, because earlier WPA card indexes to Alabama, Florida, and Louisiana are faster tools for accessing the land entry file folders. (Those three states were included in Test Question #2). The nine states with completed name indexes are sold separately as CD-ROM publications for $15.00 each, and can be obtained from the BLM office in Springfield, Virginia. A better deal, however, is a single CD-ROM produced privately which includes name indexes for eight of the eastern states. The indexes for Alabama, Arkansas, Florida, Louisiana, Michigan, Minnesota, Ohio, and Wisconsin are all available on one CD-ROM publication. (That CD can be purchased from Heritage Quest for $29.95 plus $3.50 shipping and handling. It is Heritage Quest's CD #255). The latest BLM state index completed is Mississippi, which is currently only available from the BLM office in Springfield, Virginia. For more information about CD-ROM indexes, contact the BLM Springfield office at (703) 440-1600.

Computer genealogists can access a website on the Internet devoted to the GLO Automated Project. All of the above mentioned state indexes for the Eastern Public Land states are available, and each patent can be viewed and printed. As of February 2000, only Iowa has not been indexed. Searches are done by state. Just type the name of the person you are looking for. Access the following URL: http://www.glorecords.blm.gov.

When you have received a copy of the patent, or you have located a person listed in one of the BLM indexes, you will have all of the necessary information to obtain the land entry case files from the National Archives branch in Washington, DC. The BLM name indexes include a case file number for a land transaction and the name of the land office in which the land sale took place. If you have a copy of the patent, you will find a case file number at the top of the page. In addition, the name of the Government Land Office that handled the land transaction will be given.

NOTE: If you locate a person using any of the CD-ROM indexes, it may be useful to print a copy of the page showing the name of the person and the rest of the information for that land transaction. This page can then be included with your letter of request for a patent. The print-out will give the BLM office all the information they will need to pull the patent from the files.

You can now write for a copy of NATF form 84 from:

> Old Military & Civil — Land Team
> National Archives and Records Administration,
> Washington, DC 20408.

Once you have a copy of the NATF for 84, fill out and mail the form requesting copies of the land entry files. You may Include a copy of the patent you received from the Bureau of Land Management. Or, you can copy down the case file number and the name of the land office as part of the request form.

Test Question #5

WAS THE LAND ENTRY BEFORE JANUARY 1, 1908... AND, the land entry was in the state of Iowa?

If you can answer this question with a "yes," write a letter to:

> Bureau of Land Management
> Eastern States Branch
> 7450 Boston Blvd.
> Springfield, VA 22153

No form is required. Your letter should include the following information:

- The name of the person who obtained land from the federal government.
- The state wherein the land was located.
- The exact legal description of the property. An exact legal description MUST be provided, such

as: "the northwest 1/4 section, township 24 north, range 4 east, 2nd principal meridian." The BLM staff will use the property description to locate the correct Government Land Office where the land transaction took place. Once in the correct land office records, they will find the name of the person listed as an entryman in either the plat book or tract book created by that land office. This will lead them to the case file number needed to obtain the land entry papers located at the National Archives I branch in Washington, DC. If you do not know the property description, do one of the following:

1. Get the property description from a deed in a courthouse. When the person's land was sold, a property description was recorded on the deed. The property description may be found in the grantee/grantor index to deeds in the courthouse, without having to read the deed itself.

2. Find the property description on a plat map or land ownership atlas, where the names of property owners are listed on a map for one federal township. From the map, a property description can be deduced. One page in the atlas is usually one federal township, such as "Township 24 North, Range 4. East."

3. If you have a copy of a patent for the property in question, the file number and land office is shown on the patent. If you have homestead papers, deeds, or any other reference to the land, look for the legal description which should be included in the papers.

Your letter should include a request for a copy of the PATENT issued to the person.

After you have received a copy of the patent, you will have all of the necessary information to obtain the land entry case files from the National Archives I branch in Washington, DC.

The patent has the case file number at the top right hand corner. In addition, the name of the Government Land Office that handled the land transaction will be given. With these two items, you can now write for a copy of NATF form 84 from:

> Old Military & Civil Section — Land Team
> National Archives and Records Administration
> Washington, DC 20408

Your filled-in form is for requesting copies of any land entry case files (the file folder). You may include a copy of the patent you received from the Bureau of Land Management. Or, you can copy down the case file number and the name of the land office as part of your request on the form. Access the following URL on the Internet for current information:
http://www.nara.gov/genealogy/

Essay 2

Land Grants and Deed Records

This essay first appeared as an article by William Dollarhide, "Retracing the Trails of Your Ancestors Using Deed Records" in the *Genealogy Bulletin*, No. 25 (Jan-Feb 1995).

A Ninety Percent Chance

Since the first colonists came to this continent, land ownership has always been an important part of our American society. As an example, nine out of ten adult white males in America owned land before 1850. Even today the figure is over fifty percent.

With this nearly universal coverage before 1850 and since genealogical research starts getting more difficult about that time, it is a wonder that family historians are not using land ownership records more often to solve their genealogical puzzles.

For instance, did you know that there is a surname index to virtually every land owner in America since the early 1600s — an index that is more complete than any head-of-household census index ever compiled? And did you know that you have a ninety percent chance of finding your ancestor in that land ownership index? The land ownership index is not combined into a single name list. There are thousands of them. Usually called a "Grantee-Grantor" index, one can be found in the courthouse of any of the 3,141 counties in the United States. Together, they comprise the largest index which names residents of the United States, particularly for the period 1629-1860.

There are few indexes used by genealogists that offer a ninety percent chance of finding the right person. Even today, a modern telephone directory gives the names of only those households with a publicly listed telephone number.

(A recent study in Los Angeles County revealed that about twenty percent of the telephone numbers are unlisted numbers.) Yet, there is a surname index for Los Angeles County that gives the names of ninety percent of the heads of household of that county during the 1850s and later.

Let's take the 1840 census as an example. In 1840, the names of the heads of household are all that are shown — but if you were to look at the Grantee/Grantor index for the same county, you may discover that one household could have more than one landowner. Say you find in the census that the head of household is John Smith, Jr. But, what you don't know is that living in the same household is John Smith, Sr., and maybe even John Smith, III; and each of them own a piece of property. Only John Smith, Jr. is listed in the 1840 head of household census, but the Grantee/Grantor index lists all three landowners.

We genealogists eventually recognize the significance of land ownership as we attempt to locate records of our ancestors. But, at first look, we may not see the importance of land records because they do not seem to give us the vital genealogical facts we are after, i.e., names of parents, dates, children, and so on.

But, genealogists who dig into the land records deeper will discover that land grants and deeds can provide evidence of the places where an ancestor lived and for how long, when he moved into or moved out of a county, and, in many cases, a surprising amount of detailed information about a person.

Why Land Records?

Here are three good reasons why land records are valuable for genealogical research:

1. **The odds are good.** Since 90% of the adult white male population owned land before 1850, land grants and deeds provide an excellent way of finding an ancestor in local records. Deeds are recorded at the county level; and when property is sold a deed is recorded at the local courthouse. It is a protection to both the buyer and seller that the land being transferred is properly recorded. There are exceptions, such as a deed held by a private party and never recorded — which is every title insurance agent's worst nightmare. But, deeds are almost always recorded at the courthouse of the county wherein the land is located.

2. **Land records are more complete than other records.** Land records such as property tax lists, deeds and deed indexes, and the written transcripts of real estate transactions all go back further in time than any other type of record we use in genealogical research. The earliest records in Europe, other than those recorded for the Royal Courts, are land records. For example, the Domesday Books — which are property tax lists — were first gathered for William the Conqueror in the 11th Century and are the earliest English records in which a common farmer or tradesman may be listed by name. Certain Scandinavian land records date back to 950 AD. In America, land ownership has always been important, so much so that if a courthouse were to be destroyed by fire or natural disaster, the deed records — proof of land ownership — were reconstructed by local authorities soon after. For example, deed records were reconstructed for several counties after General Sherman's troops burned courthouse after courthouse during the Civil War.

3. **Land records often reveal the name of a man's wife.** The English common law system of "dower rights" for a widow was followed in the American colonies and continued through the 19th Century. Dower rights entitled a widow to 1/3 of her husband's estate upon his death. No written will had to specify that amount. As a result of the dower rights of a married woman, early land deeds will almost always mention the name of a man's wife because she had a legal interest in any land being sold or purchased. In fact, a woman had "veto power" over the sale of land by her husband. Under the English system, a married woman could not own land in

her own name; but with her dower rights, she could veto the sale of the land. Many early deed transcripts will include an affidavit in which a wife was interviewed privately by the court clerk to determine if she was in favor of the sale or not.

State Land States vs Public Land States

Before digging into the land grants, a genealogists needs to know if his ancestor's land grant was located in a Public Land state or a State Land state.

In 1787, the United States government created the Territory Northwest of the Ohio River, and the "Public Domain" was born. Public Domain areas today comprise a total of thirty (30) states in which the federal government issued land grants. These thirty are called Public Land states.

There are a total of twenty (20) State Land states. They are the original thirteen states plus five states whose bounds were taken from the original thirteen, i.e., Vermont, Kentucky, Tennessee, Maine, and West Virginia. Upon annexation to the Union, both Texas and Hawaii retained ownership of their public lands and become State Land states.

So, twenty U.S. states retained ownership of their lands; and each set up a General Land Office for the issuing of land grants. For example, Virginia, as a State Land state, sold land directly to private individuals. But, land in Michigan, a Public Land state, was sold by the United States Federal Government.

To locate the earliest land records from the agency that sold the land, you first need to know if the land grant was located in a State Land state or a Public Land state.

Documents Relating to Original Land Grants

There are a few definitions needed for documents referenced in old deeds or land grants. These documents may give important genealogical clues about your ancestors. These are documents issued by the government agency in charge of selling land, each of the twenty State Land states, or the United States Federal Government. The use of these old documents dates back to England during the time of William the Conqueror in the latter half of the 11th Century. As part of established English land grant procedures, they were brought to the English colonies in North America and continued well into the era after the independence of the United States or Canada.

Warrant. This was the first document in the land grant process. A warrant authorizes a tract of land to be set aside for a land grant or sale. It may describe the land in general terms, such as "200 acres of land west of the New River." A government agency issued a warrant, e.g., the King of England, the Commonwealth of Massachusetts, the Proprietor of Maryland, the State of Connecticut, or the United States Federal Government if the land were located in one of the thirty Public Land states after 1787.

Warrants are records that can confirm that your ancestor did indeed receive a land grant — it is the first document in what may be several records relating to a land grant to a private party.

Special warrants were issued by colonial, state, and federal Governments as payment to soldiers for service in various wars, including the Colonial Wars of the 18th Century, the Revolutionary War, and the War of 1812. These "bounty-land" warrants indicated a certain number of acres of land without describing the land precisely. The warrant certificate had a cash value based on the location of the land and the number of acres involved. Warrants could be assigned (sold) to someone other than the person granted the warrant before the land was surveyed.

Survey. After a warrant was issued, a survey of the land was conducted, which defined the exact location and boundaries of the land grant authorized in the warrant. Before the land grant could be possessed, the boundaries of the land had to be marked on the ground. A survey might include a map or description of the boundaries of the land, and the government's surveyor may have written a statement that he had followed the provisions of the warrant.

The survey document might include the names of the surveyor's assistants, or "sworn chain bearers," who were often chosen because they lived next door to the property being surveyed. As a result, survey records often reveal genealogical clues to the neighbors of your ancestor and assist in locating the land exactly.

Patent. The final document was the title certificate (deed) that was issued to a person granted or sold land — the first private owner of land. The patent was issued by the governmental agency that originally owned the land. Reference to a patentee indicates that person holds an "original entry of land." A patent is the same as a deed, but the word patent applies to a first title holder.

Land Patents Today

The keeper of surviving land warrants, surveys, or patents today is the issuing government agency. For example, if you know your ancestor received a colonial land grant in North Carolina (a State Land state), any surviving warrants, surveys, or patents are held by the State of North Carolina and are located today at the North Carolina State Archives.

Or, if you think your ancestor obtained a land grant in Indiana (a Public Land state), the keeper of the warrants, surveys, and patents is the United States Government. U.S. Public Land Records today are under the care of the Bureau of Land Management (BLM) or the National Archives of the United States.

The procedures for locating patents and Land Entry Case Files for all thirty Public Land states is detailed in Essay 1, "Federal Land Records." Since the patent was not a document issued at the county level, it may not be obvious from local records that a man had an original entry of land. The patent did not have to be recorded at the county courthouse unless the property was sold. But, in many county courthouses, genealogists may find a book called "Original Entries of Land" which gives the names and property description for those persons who obtained original patents for land in a particular county.

There may also be voter's lists, tax lists, or county assessor's records which confirm that a person was a patent holder based on a county tax liability against his property. You may also find a county-wide "plat book" which shows the same information. A plat book is a map showing the physical location of property ownership within a particular county or region of a county. If any of these types of records survive today, they are usually located at the county courthouse for the county wherein the land was located.

Land ownership maps are another source of confirming if a man had an original entry of land. Based on county-wide plat maps and other public documents, private companies have produced land ownership maps for about half of the counties of the U.S., some as large sheets, others as bound books. The Library of Congress in Washington, DC; has the best collection of these old land ownership maps. There are two excellent guides to locate a map for a county and to determine if your ancestor's name appears on one of these land ownership maps. The first is for the manuscript maps (sheets) located in the Library of Congress: Richard W. Stephenson, compiler, *Land Ownership Maps: A Checklist of Nineteenth Century United States County Maps in the Library of Congress* (Washington, DC: Geography and Map Division, Reference Department, Library of Congress, 1967); and another guide is a checklist of the land ownership maps found in bound atlases: *Land Ownership Atlases in the Library of Congress* (Washington, DC: Library of Congress, 1981). The latter is a county-by-county index to the various land ownership maps published as atlases. To obtain copies of these maps, write to the Library of Congress and specify the name of the county in which you have an interest and the time period. Mention the two sources for land ownership maps. Write to **Library of Congress, Photo-duplication Services, Washington, DC 20540.** The staff will determine if such a map or atlas exists and will quote you a price for making copies of the maps for you.

Subsequent Exchanges of Land

After a patent had been issued to a landowner, he had the right to sell the land to someone else in the form of a deed; but the recording of such land sales became a local responsibility. Unlike the warrants, surveys, or patents, which were recorded at the state or federal level, exchanges of land subsequent to the land grant process are recorded at the county level. This is true for all states except three New England states where the deeds are recorded at the town level (Connecticut, Rhode Island, and Vermont), and Alaska (the only state with no counties and where land exchanges are recorded at the Judicial District level.) In Louisiana, deeds are recorded at a parish courthouse which is the same as a county courthouse in other states.

Some definitions related to land exchanges at the county or town level are as follows:

Deed. This is the private document which records that the ownership of a parcel of land was transferred from one party to another. A copy of the deed is recorded in the county or town wherein the land is located, even though the sale of land may have taken place somewhere else. The deed certificate then acts as the title to property in the possession of the buyer. There are several types of deeds such as Warranty Deeds, Trust Deeds, or Quit Claim Deeds, all of which may be used to transfer or relinquish a claim to property.

Grantor. The party selling or relinquishing land.

Grantee. The party buying or being granted land.

Grantor/Grantee Index. The index to private land exchanges. In some counties it may be called the Direct (grantor) Index and Indirect (grantee) Index. Or, it may be called the Index to Real Estate Conveyances. The format of the index is virtually the same in all counties of the U.S. It is a general alphabetized list of the sellers of land and buyers of land. A Grantor/Grantee index is a valuable genealogical resource. Before 1850, for example, a Grantor/Grantee was a better list of the residents of a county than a heads-of-household census for the same county.

Genealogical Research in Deed Records

Research in county/town deed records requires that you have access to the Grantor/Grantee Index and then access to the deed books which provide a written record of a land transaction. There are two noteworthy books that list every county in the U.S., and the name of the office which maintains the land records. The most popular is *The Handy Book for Genealogists* (Logan, UT: Everton Publishers, Inc., 9th Edition, 1999). However, the Handy Book omits land records data for many counties and does not list the New England towns. A more complete review of the county offices can be found under "Land Records" for every state in *The Red Book: American State, County & Town Sources*, edited by Alice Eichholz, Ph.D. C.G., (Salt Lake City: Ancestry, Inc., 1992). *The Red Book* lists every county as well as an address for each of the New England towns, including the three states where deeds are recorded at the town level: Connecticut, Rhode Island, and Vermont.

There are three (3) ways you can conduct research in deed records:

1. **Research at the courthouse.** The best way is to travel to the county courthouse and read the deed books yourself. The next best method is to try contacting a local genealogical society to see if there is a person who can visit the courthouse in your behalf. There may be a small fee or donation to the society, but this is an ideal way of locating another amateur genealogist to look up items for you in a courthouse. An address list of genealogical societies can be found in the *Genealogist's Address Book*, by Elizabeth Petty Bentley, (Baltimore: Genealogical Publishing Co., Inc., 1999).

2. **Research by mail.** A county's registrar of deed records may look in a deed index for you if your request is concise and to the point. Write to the keeper of deeds and ask for a check of the Grantee/Grantor Index for evidence of your ancestor's name during a period of about twenty years, enclosing a Self Address Stamped Envelope (SASE). The index will indicate the book and page number for a deed transcript — with the exact citation, write again and ask for copies of the deeds themselves, enclosing an appropriate fee.

3. **Research Microfilm copies of the deeds.** The Family History Library of The Church of Jesus Christ of Latter-day Saints has microfilmed deed records for over 1,500 counties in the U.S. Check the FHL's Internet site at www.familysearch.org, or, visit a local Family History Center to check the library's catalog to confirm the existence of microfilmed deed indexes and deed transcripts. These can be borrowed for a small fee and used at the local center, or catch a plane for Salt Lake City.

A Check List for Deed Research

- A county must be known first. Since deeds are recorded at the county level, you must have at least a clue as to the county where your ancestor lived. The exceptions are land records in Connecticut, Rhode Island, and Vermont, where deeds are recorded at the Town level.

- Come prepared with census or tax lists to find the names of the neighbors of your ancestor. It helps to have the names of other people who you know lived near your ancestor. This is a way of confirming that you are in the right place, by looking for the other names in the same area. In some cases, reading the deeds for neighbors may turn up your ancestor's name as a witness, confirming you are in the right courthouse.

- Start with the Grantee/Grantor index. Write down the name, date, deed book, and page number for every deed indexed. If you are looking for a William Johnson and know that he had a brother, Thomas Johnson, it may be important to look for all siblings' deeds as well.

- In addition to your ancestor's full name, look for "et al" after the same surname in the index ("et al" is Latin for "and others") which may indicate a group of heirs. This was used as a short-cut for a clerk writing a deed index entry in which there were more than one name for the grantors or grantees, such as "Thomas Johnson, et al." If your ancestor's name was William Johnson, he may be mentioned in the deed transcript along with Thomas Johnson — but the index may only show "Thomas Johnson, et al."

- Read each deed. Note that each will give the *place of residence* for the grantor and the grantee — this is valuable information. Before 1900, deeds usually give the county or town of residence; but today you can find an exact street address for both the grantor and grantee, right down to the zip code.

- Locate the Probate Office at the same time your are in a courthouse. You may come across a reference to a probate in a deed. The relationship between deeds and probates is that deeds to heirs may be recorded as a result of a probate judgement. In some cases, you may find a reference to a probate case file number in a deed transcript which is a back-door index to the probate files.

- Locate the Civil Court office at the same time you are in a courthouse. Before 1850, the subject of over half of the lawsuits in America had something to do with land disputes. A deed transcript may give you a back-door index to a civil court case and may even give you a case file number.

- Get a USGS (7.5 series) Topographical map of the area or see if the County Engineer's office has detailed maps available. (See Essay 3 for information about obtaining maps from USGS.

A CASE STUDY: The search for Philip Reynolds

To demonstrate the power of deeds in retracing the trail of an ancestor, I will present a case study of one of my own ancestors. This is a real example of the use of deeds to solve a difficult genealogical problem. If you have the problem of knowing that an ancestor was from Virginia, but do not know in which county he lived, then this example may give you an idea of how deeds can help you locate the right county. Remember, we are basing this research on the fact that there is a ninety percent chance that your ancestor owned land. Let's see if we can solve a "needle in the haystack" search for an ancestor when all we know is that he was born in Virginia in about 1788.

The steps I followed to locate the right county using deeds has been repeated several times. My first success was for an ancestor named Philip Reynolds. To follow along, I will have to give you some of my own genealogy — but any genealogist should be able to relate his own situation to this example.

The problem:

Where exactly did Philip Reynolds live before 1830? In Indiana? In Ohio? In Virginia? Where was he married? Who were his parents?......Does this problem sound familiar?

Facts known, in the order they were found:

1. John Dollarhide, and family living in Jasper County, Indiana, per 1850 census. Apparent wife, Lucy, born in Ohio about 1821. A Philip Reynolds living with them, born c1788 in Virginia. (I had only a guess about who Philip Reynolds might be...)

2. John Dollarhide head of household, 1840 census of Tippecanoe County, Indiana.

3. John Dollarhide married a Lucy Reynolds, 1836, in Tippecanoe County, Indiana, based on a copy of their marriage record. This was the first confirmation that her maiden name was Reynolds. I returned to the 1850 census to look at Philip Reynolds with renewed interest.

4. Philip Reynolds head of household, 1840 census of Tippecanoe County, Indiana, not too far from John Dollarhide household.

5. Philip Reynolds, head of household, 1830 census of Tippecanoe County, Indiana. Several females of right age to be Lucy Reynolds.

6. 1820 Ohio Census Index: only two (2) heads of households with the name Philip Reynolds — one in Trumbull County, the other in Miami County. The Miami County family seemed most promising, but no way to prove which was the right family.

7. Obituary from a Corvallis, Oregon newspaper, dated 1878, stated, "Philip Reynolds was born in Virginia . . . he married Sophia Hill . . . they lived in Ohio a number of years . . . and were the parents of nine children". This obit also mentioned a surviving daughter, one Lucy Dollarhide, living in California.

8. Philip Reynolds was living with a daughter in Oregon, per 1870 census, born c1788 in Virginia.

9. Philip Reynolds living with another daughter in Iowa, per 1860 census, born c1788 in Virginia.

I might mention that Philip Reynolds has become one my favorite ancestors. It appears that after his wife died in about 1843, the man never worked again — he just moved in with a daughter until she couldn't stand it any more and then moved to another daughter's home. I found him living with three different daughters in census records, and since he had nine daughters, his average stay with each lasted only three to four years. In all, he managed to live off his kids for nearly thirty-five years. I have decided that this is a man I would like to emulate.

Confirmation needed:

Was Miami County the place to start? Or perhaps Trumbull County first?

Course of Action:

- Checked library sources for Trumbull and Miami County, Ohio, for any reference to Reynolds family about 1820. Nothing found for Philip.

- Checked printed court records for both counties. No Philip.

- Checked county histories for both counties. Philip not mentioned.

- Borrowed LDS library microfilm for Deeds (Grantee/Grantor books) for Miami County, Ohio, for the period 1810-1830. This was based on my knowledge that Lucy (Reynolds) Dollarhide was born in Ohio about 1821.

NOTE: I decided to go through the deeds from Miami County first. This seemed logical because the Philip Reynolds in Trumbull County appeared in the 1820, 1830, and 1840 censuses (and my Philip was in Indiana in 1830). The Philip Reynolds listed in Miami County was there in 1820 but not in the 1830 or 1840 censuses.

After thoroughly reading the Miami County Grantor/Grantee index, I found that the only Philip Reynolds mentioned was in a single transaction that took place in 1837. Since I knew that Philip was in Indiana by 1830, I stopped here. From the index, I obtained the following:

Miami County, Ohio
Deed Book 15, page 355 — Date deed recorded: 22 Sep 1837
Grantor: Philip Reynolds
Grantee: Joseph R. John

There were two things wrong with the deed. First, I expected a deed in which Sophia's name was mentioned, since dower rights were still in play in Ohio in the 1830's. I expected to see, "Philip

Reynolds and wife Sophia..." as a grantor or grantee in the deeds. Second, the date was all wrong. I knew that my Philip Reynolds was in Indiana in 1837 and here was a deed in Ohio for well after the time Philip Reynolds moved to Indiana. But, as I was to learn later, I was not paying attention.

First Breakthrough!

On a trip through Salt Lake City, I decided to visit the Family History Library and look up that same Reynolds deed just for the fun of it. Book 15 of the Miami county deeds had been microfilmed. On page 355, I found the following deed recorded:

"...*Philip Reynolds, of Indiana, to Joseph R. John, of Troy, Miami County, Ohio, lot 151, for $60.00...*"

The deed gave Philip Reynolds' residence! I was now convinced that this was indeed my Philip Reynolds of Tippecanoe County, Indiana. But why wasn't Sophia's name mentioned? I have since learned that the dower rights for a wife did not apply to small parcels of land (under one acre or so), so there was no need for Sophia's name to be part of the deed. It was also clear that Philip Reynolds had owned land in Miami County, Ohio, but did not get around to selling his lot in the town of Troy until some years after moving to Indiana.

Since I had several census records giving Philip Reynolds's birth as Virginia about 1788, I wondered if it were possible to use this same technique to find the right county in Virginia to search for the Reynolds family. I canceled everything else on my agenda, booked five more days in Salt Lake City, and headed for the microfilmed Virginia deed records. It was now "needle in a haystack" time, but which county first?

Second Breakthrough!

I needed to narrow down the number of counties of Virginia to start my search for Philip Reynolds. There were 135 counties in Virginia in 1820, which included present-day West Virginia. So, I first went through the 1800 and 1810 censuses (actually, reconstructed tax lists) for Virginia looking for the name Reynolds. None of the heads of household had the name Philip Reynolds.

But, there were eighteen (18) different counties with both the surname Reynolds and Hill. (Sophia's maiden name was Hill. I decided to look in just those counties which had evidence of both of these surnames.)

I decided to check the Grantor-Grantee index to all eighteen counties, for the period 1790-1830. I began in alphabetical order and discovered that I could go through a whole county in a matter of minutes to determine if a Philip Reynolds ever owned land there. I was in the Bedford County, Virginia, Grantor-Grantee index and found this information:

Bedford County, Virginia
Deed Book 18, page 359
Date: 15 May 1824
Grantor: Philip and Sophia Reynolds
Grantee: Charles Bayman

I was immediately out of my chair to get the microfilmed Bedford County deeds to read the complete transcript. Here is how the deed transcript began:

"...This Indenture made this 15ᵗʰ day of May A.D. 1824 between Philip Reynolds and Sophia his wife of the County of Miami, and the state of Ohio of the one part and Charles Bayman of the County of Bedford, Virginia...."

No doubt about it! This was the right couple, and the right county in Virginia! Once I had established Bedford County, Virginia, as the county where Philip and Sophia Reynolds lived, less than thirty minutes later I was in Bedford County marriage records, where I found the following entry:

"Philip Reynolds to Sophia Hill, 20 Dec 1806"

Summary: Without using deeds, it would have been possible to find Philip Reynolds in Miami County, Ohio, or Bedford County, Virginia — but using the deed indexes as a finding tool, it was quicker and easier to get to the right place. Other records soon became apparent, and the research task was a huge success. What I was able to do with the deeds was retrace the trail Philip Reynolds followed from Virginia to Ohio, and to Indiana. Without the deed in Ohio, I would not have been able to confirm that the deed in Virginia was for the same man.

This example of using deeds to establish the trail an ancestor followed is not a rare occurrence. Every deed will give you the residence of both the grantor and grantee. If a man sold his land after leaving a county, you may learn of the place he moved to. If a man bought land in another county before moving, you may learn the name of the county he left. If a man owned several parcels of land in a county, the first deed and the last deed may provide important evidence of the exact dates of a person's residence in a particular place.

Why Not Look at Deeds First?

I used to check land records only after going through every published source for a county. I have discovered that deed records can provide the most important information we need in genealogical research: the place where a person lived. I now do deed research first, not last. Here are three reasons why:

1. Deeds are usually indexed in cumulative form, sometimes spanning over decades. They may be listed in only a few large volumes, while marriages and other county records may be spread across many, many volumes. Going through the grantee-grantor indexes does not take as long as going through other records.

2. For early periods, deed indexes act as a list of residents in a county to give you a good review of who lived there, including neighbors you have noted from census or tax lists. It is a way of getting a "yes" or "no" answer to the question of the right county where a person lived. It is an excellent way to retrace the trail your ancestor followed. This is based on a ninety percent chance that your ancestor owned land. If a man is not listed in a deed index, the chances are great that he did not live in that county.

3. Deed indexes sometimes make reference to a "case number" for some civil action regarding property or a probate court action. Probate and civil court case files are excellent sources of genealogical information — but poorly indexed. Therefore, going through the deeds first may present the only clue that other records exist in another part of the courthouse.

Quit-Claim Deeds and Deed Releases

Another type of deed is known as a "quit-claim deed." This type of conveyance is used for transferring property when an issue of ownership might not be clear. Essentially, a quit-claim deed says, "...I hereby relinquish (quit) any interest I may have in this property..."

There are actual examples of the Brooklyn Bridge being sold through the use of Quit Claim deeds. This deed is a legal document, but all it says is that a person is releasing his interest in property. A Quit-Claim deed does not prove that a person actually owned the property.

In recorded land records, Quit-Claim deeds often reveal genealogical information. They were often used by lawyers who were attempting to clear title on a piece of property and to avoid the possibility of a claim against it.

A common use was when a person died without a will and the probate court needed to establish the legal heirs of the deceased land owner. Quit-Claim deeds might be recorded for any person suspected of having an interest in the property. Here is where you may learn of a grandson, niece, or nephew of deceased person. Some of the relatives may have filed a Quit-Claim deed relinquishing their interest in the property of the deceased.

A similar record is called a "deed release," which is used in about the same way as a Quit-Claim deed. Both of these types of deeds are normally indicated in the "Type of Conveyance" column in the Grantee/Grantor index. Genealogists will find these two special types of deeds particularly interesting because they very often provide you with relationships. A release of claim to property between brothers and sisters, for example, is a common occurrence in land records.

Examples of Quit Claim Deeds

In doing research on my Rumbaugh family of Fulton County, Indiana, the Grantee/Grantor index had a very simple line that read, "William Rumbaugh, et al". Going to the book and page in the deed book led me to eight (8) Quit-Claim Deeds, all for the same date in 1856, all in the same hand, and all starting with this type of phrase:

"...William Rumbaugh, heir of David Rumbaugh, Deceased, and Susan Holton (formerly Rumbaugh), of this County, does Quit any Claim to the land described as..."

"...Nancy Wiles, intermarried with William Wiles, and an heir of David Rumbaugh, Deceased, and Susan Holton (formerly Rumbaugh), of Union County, Iowa, does Quit any Claim to the land described as..."

...and another entry for each of the rest of the brothers and sisters...

The use of Quit-Claim deeds, in this case, was a convenient way for the heirs of David Rumbaugh to transfer their share of the inheritance to just one of the brothers. Even though David Rumbaugh's will devised the property to each of the heirs equally, the heirs decided later to combine the property back again for a home for one family.

Because of this land-swapping, a complete list of the heirs of David Rumbaugh was found — not in the probate office, and not even in the family Bible. The list of children was taken from the Deed Books of Fulton County, Indiana!

After Finding a Deed

With a deed in hand, you always have a property description. That means that a map showing the exact location of that property could be found next. With a map as a guide, locate and mark the spot for the land. Now look for the nearest cemetery on the map. (How about the nearest Church?) Now find the records for that cemetery or church. A map can also give clues about the location of the land in relation to the courthouse of that county. Was the courthouse for an adjoining county closer to the family farm? If the family members could travel more easily to a different courthouse (for a marriage license, perhaps), you may have some more research options.

Essay 2: Land Grants and Deed Records

Maps, Names, and Places

This essay first appeared as an article by William Dollarhide, "Maps, Names, and Places" in the *Genealogy Bulletin*, No. 39 (May-June 1997)

Name Collectors

Genealogical researchers are name collectors. We collect names of people and names of places. When a name of a person can be connected to a name of a place and a time period, the research really starts paying off. Here is an example. If you wanted to find records for a James Johnson in America, how many possibilities are there? From 1607, the date of the first English settlement in America at Jamestown, Virginia, to 2000 is 393 years. How many persons with the name James Johnson have lived in America in 393 years? Clearly, we need to refine the information if we want to find the right James Johnson.

If we could say the life-span of James Johnson was estimated to be "between 1800 and 1870," we could cut the number of years from 393 to 70. And, if we could further determine that James Johnson lived in Boston during his lifetime, we could reduce the numbers even more. The more information we know, the greater we can reduce the possibilities for a person named James Johnson.

Possibility of locating information for a person named James Johnson, if he...	Possible Number
...lived in America between 1800 and 1870	5,600
...lived in Massachusetts between 1800 and 1870	424
...lived in Boston between 1800 and 1870	156
...lived in Boston in 1850	23
...lived in Boston in 1850 on Thacher Street	1

So, a key element in genealogical research is the process of locating the exact place where an ancestors lived. If we can locate the exact place of residence for a person back in time, we can locate the records they left there. We know, for example, that finding the county of residence for an ancestor opens the door to the myriad of resource materials in local courthouses, libraries, city directories, funeral homes, cemeteries, and so on.

Why Every Genealogist Needs a Good Map

Genealogical researchers need a highly detailed map showing the region where an ancestor lived. The map becomes a tremendous tool in locating place-names, cemeteries, churches, nearby towns, post offices, and the terrain and roads your ancestor may have known years ago. It is remarkable that there have been very few name changes to features found on a current map. Town or city names may have changed; but usually, the name of a mountain, valley, or stream never changes. Therefore, the names of places found on a current topographic map are just as good as having a 200-year-old map. A detailed map provides a real education to a researcher concerning the lay of the land where an ancestor lived.

Undoubtably the best maps for genealogical research are the USGS 7.5 series topographical maps which cover virtually every inhabited place in America. The 7.5 designation represents 7-1/2 minutes of one degree of latitude and longitude. Depending on the spot on the globe, this area is a rectangle which is about 6-7 miles across by 7-8 miles deep. The area of coverage on one of these maps is called a "quadrangle."

The 7.5 topographic maps show this area at a scale of 1:24,000. This is the same as saying "one inch on the map is equal to 24,000 inches on the ground." Each printed map sheet of the 7.5 series is about 24 by 30 inches in size. To give you an idea of how much detail can be seen on a 1:24,000 map, a square inch on the map is approximately 92 acres of land on the ground. A half-inch square would be about 23 acres, and a quarter-inch square would represent a little less than six acres. The 7.5 series maps are beautifully printed in seven colors, and they are an outstanding value.

With such great map detail, one can see virtually every stream or river, every hill or valley, the streets within every town or city, and even the buildings in a town. In addition, the maps show obscure features, such as cemeteries, churches, back country roads, trails, mines, or ponds. If a feature on the map has a name, that information is given as well.

Hence, a researcher can locate Toad Lake in Whatcom County, Washington; Dollarhide Swamp in Greene County, Alabama; or Braddock Heights in Frederick County, Maryland; or hundreds of thousands of other named features. Over 55,000 topographic map sheets have been produced for the 7.5 series, covering most of the United States. At this scale, it would take a wall 300 feet high and 460 feet wide to display the entire U.S. as one map.

With an average of 35 named features on each of the 55,000 sheets, the full list adds up to over 1.5 million place-names in the U.S. The only areas of the country not covered at the 1:24,000 scale are some mountain regions or areas with no agriculture or population.

The next best map series is the USGS 15 minute series. But, one 24" x 30" sheet of the 15 minute series covers four times the area of the 7.5 series maps. Thus, it takes four maps sheets at the 7.5 series to cover the same area of one 15 minute map sheet. However, for certain areas not covered in the 7.5 series, the 15 minute series maps may offer a reasonable substitute. The 15 minute series covers 100% of the U.S., including all uninhabited mountains and deserts.

Finding Great-Grandfather's Farm on a Map

Genealogists involved in land and property research in America may already know the value of the USGS 7.5 series maps. The range/township divisions in the thirty public-land states are used for all legal descriptions in those states. After a researcher has identified an ancestor's property described in a deed at a local courthouse, a USGS 7.5 quadrangle map should then be obtained. Since the range/township lines are prominently shown on the 7.5 maps, a researcher can easily determine the exact location of any piece of property, right down to a five-acre plot of land. Therefore, it is possible to precisely locate great-grandfather's farm on a map.

In the twenty state-land states with metes and bounds surveys, a 7.5 series topographic map is also an excellent way to locate an ancestor's property. Since most of the metes and bounds deed descriptions start with a water course, it is important in these land descriptions to first locate a river, creek, or stream. With the detail shown on a 7.5 quadrangle map, watercourses are easy to find because they are all named on the maps. It is quite possible to plot on the 7.5 series maps an irregular property description as small as five or ten acres in size. Metes and bounds property descriptions can be squares, rectangles, parallelograms, or polygons (five or more sides). Once you have located the starting point of the property description, each side of the plotted diagram requires a compass reading for an angle and a distance measurement for the length of each side, usually in feet.

For genealogy purposes, the topographic map becomes a powerful tool. Once an exact property site has been located on a detailed map, a genealogist can learn the answers to some very important questions, such as: where is the nearest cemetery? Where is the nearest church? Where is the nearest town? How far is it to the county seat? Is there a mountain or river that acts as a barrier to the county seat? Is it closer to travel to an adjoining county seat? What are the names of various features near the ancestor's property? Are any of the names familiar? Where are the roads to or near the property?

How to Obtain a Topographic Map from USGS

The USGS has a toll-free phone: 1-800-ASK-USGS (1-888-275-8747). This number is the USGS toll-free general information number and will give you the correct office for information and another 1-800 number for ordering maps. Through their voice-mail options, this number will allow you to reach a live person who can answer any of your questions about USGS maps, plus take an order for any of their special publications.

First, you should use this 800 number to ask for the "Index to Map Coverage" for any or all of the 50 states. There is an index for each state in the form of a booklet (or a large folded index map showing the same information). The USGS will mail you a state-wide index to map coverage at no charge. Your tax dollars paid for its printing. So, get some of it back by asking for the free index booklet/map for any state in which you have an interest.

The index conveniently grids a state into sections so a particular quadrangle can be located. Each quadrangle has a name; and since you cannot order unless you know the name of the quadrangle you want from USGS, the index is absolutely necessary. Be sure to refer to the "7.5 series" when you ask for the index to map coverage. Any single map sheet can be ordered for a price of $4.00. In addition, USGS charges a shipping and handling fee of $3.50 per order.

At the same time you ask for the "Index to Map Coverage," ask for some other free publications. For each state, there is a booklet called a "Catalog of Published Maps." This catalog is the best way to learn what other USGS maps may be available for each state. For example, the Mississippi River has been mapped in great detail, showing every bend of the river, every named point, and every little island. Use the state-wide catalog to learn about other interesting maps that can be obtained. Every state catalog includes a listing of United States base maps, another useful series of maps for genealogists because they show all counties for all states. My favorite is "Base Map of the U.S., No. 2B" which shows all streams and rivers, counties, county seats, and major cities. This particular U.S. base map is in two sections, about 48" x 96" in size, and costs about $10.00. The catalog booklet also gives the current prices for the various series of maps, as well as USGS forms for ordering maps through the mail.

Another USGS publication is just for genealogists. In response to the great number of genealogists asking about maps, the USGS has produced a little booklet, "Using Maps in Genealogy." This is a nicely-done guide to the use of maps and contains an excellent bibliography of books, maps, and atlases. Ask for a copy when you call for the index catalog. It's free.

USGS On-Line

Genealogical researchers can access the USGS agency's website on the Internet. I reached the site in less then a minute by using the Yahoo browser and the following key words: U.S. Government — U.S. Geological Survey — Mapping. Once I landed at their website, I found their address to be http://mapping.usgs.gov/esic/prices/maps.html

Earth Science Information Centers

The USGS sponsors Earth Science Information Centers (ESIC) around the country. These facilities are open to the public and stock a large quantity of USGS maps, particularly for the region in which they are located. There may be one close to your home; and if so, you can purchase any of the USGS maps in person. You can locate an ESIC by checking a local telephone book under U.S. Government, U.S. Geological Survey — Earth Science Information Center. Each ESIC office will have the 7.5 series topographic maps for the region in which they are located and will take orders for any map coverage for the rest of the country.

In addition to the ESIC offices for purchasing maps, the USGS website may give you the address for a commercial map dealer in your area. You may pay more for the maps through private map dealers, but the very map you want may be just down the street from your house. The USGS 7.5 series maps are often found at retail businesses that cater to outdoor sports and recreation

Geographic Names Information System

For the past several years, the USGS has been extracting place-names from maps and entering them into computers. Their goal has been to produce the *National Gazetteer of the United States*, an alphabetized listing of every named place or topographic feature that exists in the United States. The *Gazetteer* has not yet been published. An early version of this Phase I database was published in eleven volumes by OmniGraphics, Inc., of Detroit, Michigan. Seen mostly in larger libraries, the cost to purchase the printed OmniGraphics gazetteer is over $1,200. But the same list of place-names can be now be accessed at no charge on the Internet.

Phase I of the gazetteer project was to extract the place-names from the 7.5 series maps, which is now complete for all fifty states and all U.S. possessions. Phase II of the project is well under way. It adds place-names from historical maps, post office maps, old road maps, old gazetteers, and any other known place-name source. Only a few states have been completed through the Phase II stage.

Even though the project is not completed yet, the names that have been compiled and computerized so far comprise an enormous database of place-names. USGS calls this database the Geographic Names Information System (GNIS). Recently, the huge GNIS place-name index was added to the USGS Internet site. So, it is now possible to search for a place by name from the nearly two million place-names in the United States. The URL to access the GNIS search is as follows: http://mapping.usgs.gov/www/gnis/gnisform.html.

Once you have located a place from the GNIS, you may display and print a map at various scales. The maps are not nearly as good as the printed sheets available through the mail, but they do offer a good look at any region of the U.S., and the service is free.

Essay 4

Organizing the Paper

This essay first appeared as an article by William Dollarhide, "Genealogical Record Keeping" in the *Genealogy Bulletin*, No. 36 (Nov-Dec 1996). It also appeared in *Heritage Quest* magazine with some revisions as "Solving the Paper Collecting Problem" in issue No. 84 (Nov-Dec 1999).

Piles of paper

When people first get interested in their family history, they are not fully prepared for what is about to happen to them. Genealogy is an addiction. New genealogists discover that they now have to do this hobby for the rest of their lives!

The first few weeks of intense genealogical research turns what used to be lovely, well-ordered persons into compulsive, determined zealots with only one thing on their minds — get that genealogy stuff! Husbands go night after night without their dinner, children are left to fend for themselves, and relatives begin answering their phone with, "Oh, it's you again... but I thought I already told you everything I know."

It is a genealogical fact of life that something strange happens to nice people — they lose control of their lives. Those of you who are just starting out in genealogy and have not learned this yet should put this book away NOW. I would not want to be the one who caused you to spend the rest of your life looking for dead relatives.

But, if you are already hooked and have a large collection of paper that is taking over your house — then you should stay with us. I will try to give you some ideas for organizing your genealogical records (otherwise known as "piles of paper").

The Paper Problem

Aside from the irritating experience of discovering that some of your ancestors had no parents (your ancestor just appeared on the planet one day), perhaps the most common problem experienced by genealogists is the stack of paper that begins to collect. As the paper pile grows, genealogists move gradually from a file tray to a series of file trays; to a file cabinet, then several file cabinets; and some may lose of several rooms of their house to the mountain of paper.

I once described my genealogy collection as "those piles of paper." If this description is not completely foreign to you, then you may be interested in how I found a way to organize that mess. My first success with organizing my genealogy mess came after a disaster. In 1974, after about two years of doing genealogy, most of my paper files were neatly stacked (in manageable piles) on a drafting table built from saw horses and a flat door. When one of the saw horses collapsed, one end of the table came crashing down and scattered all of my two-years of genealogy all over the room. My experience of picking up the paper from the floor caused me to begin developing a method of organizing that mess.

So, if you truly want to get organized too, then I suggest that you start by throwing your entire paper collection into one large pile in the center of a room. With that done, let's see how you can pick up your papers, and in what order. But first, let's identify what is in that pile of paper.

What's in the Pile?

When you first started in genealogy, you could put everything you had in one neat 3-ring binder. It wasn't long before it took several binders, then file cabinets. . . and you know the rest. When the collection was small, you could have marriage certificates, photos, pedigree charts, family group sheets, notes you had taken, copies from censuses, etc., all together in the same small notebook. In fact, if you dumped the contents of the small notebook into one pile of paper, you would still only have a small pile. Now multiply that small pile by the number of years you have been doing genealogy, and dump the contents of your file cabinets, boxes, etc., into one pile. You would find that the entire pile can be broken down into different categories of paper. So, let's start by separating the sheets of paper in the large pile into categories. We only need to identify three. And, your first step in organizing the one large pile of paper is to turn it into three piles of paper.

Category 1— Notes and Documents for Genealogical Events

This category will have the largest number of sheets of paper. It contains the photocopies of pages from books, copies of census extracts, birth certificates, marriage licenses, deeds you have copied, and so on. The paper in this category pertains to all of your families and many different surnames. This is the heart of your genealogical research. This category has the raw research notes, documents, and copies of any source that mentions your ancestors.

The nature of this category has to do with the way we do research on our ancestry. We identify genealogical events for each person who appears on our pedigree charts. Information about an individual person is gathered and recorded first, in the form of notes and documents. Then we use a family group sheet and pedigree chart to put the facts all together. Family group sheets and pedigree charts are the genealogical *presentation* of our family tree. The facts we collect before these forms are prepared represent the genealogical research for our family tree. The facts gained in genealogical *research* are almost always oriented towards one person, with the collection of facts about that person's life, or the genealogical events for a single person.

Of course, we want to link people together as married couples, as members of a family, or the blood-line connection of a person to his parents, grandparents, and so on. But, remember that all of the presentation work must be preceded by the gathering of documentation. The most important part of genealogical work, therefore, is the research to identify the significant genealogical milestones for individuals. From a collection of these facts, a family can be put together or a pedigree chart can be extended.

The significant genealogical milestones of a person's life begin with a birth. A date and place of birth is followed by a date and place of marriage, and ends with a date and place of burial. But, in-between these basic vital statistics are a myriad of events in a person's life. We are talking about *recorded* events which include anything that happened in a person's life that can be recalled from memory or from written accounts. These include, for example, a baptism, christening, or an event in which a person was recorded in history for some noteworthy deed — good or bad. The day someone entered school is a genealogical event, as is the graduation day. A name of a person mentioned in an obituary as a survivor is a genealogical event, perhaps confirming a date and place where a person lived, as well as a relationship to the deceased. In addition, an event such as a land record showing the residence for a person and the date of the land transaction is a genealogical event. Any written account of a person, however slight, is a genealogical event and adds valuable knowledge about a person's life.

All along the time-line of a person's life are events that confirm that a person lived in a particular place at a particular time. If a chronological listing of all of the events in a person's life were possible, it would give a biographical account of a person's day-by-day existence; plus it would identify all of the places a person lived. Such a complete listing is not possible unless someone has kept detailed diary entries every day for an entire lifetime. But, many of the recorded events of a person's life exist, even though they may not be obvious. For example, a record of a person's school attendance may still exist; or a record of the first piece of property a person owned exists in the form of a recorded deed in a county courthouse. A genealogist's job is to find these recorded events and extract them using the same techniques a detective uses. But, these diligent activities will make this category of paper very large.

This first category could be called your "database." This is a paper database of facts about your ancestors, and no computer is required — not yet anyway. After separating this category from the others, your goal should be to have every fact you have ever found on your ancestors in one group titled: The Notes and Documents.

If you have facts in your memory that have never been written down, now is the time to do that. The Notes and Documents category is going to be your complete database of information. And, later, we are going to organize it in such a manner that your will be able to find any particular piece of paper in seconds! For now, just get every one of the sheets of paper that belong in the Notes and Documents category separated from the other two categories. Then leave them in the middle of the floor.

Category 2 — Compiled Sheets

This second category includes any family group sheets, pedigree charts, surname lists, descendancies, or any compiled genealogical information that derives from different sources. Most of these sheets of paper were compiled by you. The information on them came from the notes and documents you have collected. They are different from the Notes and Documents category because they are compiled sheets, not original documents or notes you collect. If you want to organize them, they should be separated from the notes and documents.

Dealing with the paper to be separated into the Compiled Sheets category will not be difficult. You can put family group sheets in one notebook or file folder, for example. The same is possible with pedigree charts and descendancies. But, you cannot organize these types of records very well if they are interfiled with the other categories. After all of these materials are separated from the rest, you may want to organize this category first, because it will probably be the easiest to do.

Make file folders or notebooks to separate the various types of sheets in this category such as family group sheets, pedigree charts, and others. When you are done, take your entire family out to McDonalds to celebrate your incredible achievement. For now, ignore that still very large pile of paper that is in the middle of your kitchen. (If you have dogs or cats, you might want to cover it with plastic wrap.)

Category 3 — Research Aids

This category does not necessarily give names of people but is important to your research project because it includes "how to" items, lists of libraries in Ohio (because you have an interest in Ohio research), maps, lists of professional genealogists, societies, clubs, commercial vendors, etc. This category also includes your personal library of books pertaining to genealogical research and, of course, would include back issues of *Heritage Quest*, *The Genealogical Helper*, and other magazines.

Items in the Research Aids category are not difficult to organize. You can simply start file folders to collect all of the things that relate to Ohio and label the file "Ohio." You will find that the majority of the Research Aids category can be organized by its geographic origin, e.g., libraries in Indiana, lists of genealogists in Ohio, how to do research in South Carolina, and so on. Research books will be easily organized by being placed on a bookshelf. However, if any of your books contain information about your families, you need to copy those pages from the books and include the copies with the Notes and Documents category.

You should be able to organize all of your Research Aids (or call it your "personal library") in no time at all. These materials seem to sort themselves by place. So, to get some quick gratification, get the Research Aids organized along with the second category, Compiled Sheets; and you will be left with just one large pile of paper.

Understanding the Problem

With category two and three done, you have accomplished a great deal. You will have your compiled sheets in order, and you will have your research library in order. But you still have the first category, Notes and Documents, which is a very large pile of paper. In this pile are notes and documents on everyone you have collected. You have your paternal side of the family as well as the maternal side of the family in there. Before we take on this awesome task, let's define the reasons that are causing this category to be so difficult to organize.

As it turns out, you can not really organize the Notes and Documents category until they are separated from the other two categories — so just leave them in the middle of the room as a neat stack of paper until you have the first two categories done. Before wading into the Notes and

Documents, reward yourself with a large hot chocolate sundae for having done such a marvelous job of it so far. It would be advisable that before starting on the Notes and Documents that you have at least a 24 hour break, and a full night's rest. The next steps get harder.

Two Serious Problems Resulting from the Nature of Genealogical Research

Problem One: We have as our goal in genealogy the job of identifying families.

We are taught very early that a family group sheet is our worksheet and everything we do should be based on the family group. The fact is, we do not start with a family group sheet — we start with genealogical events for individuals. The reason so many genealogist's notes and documents need help is that they are trapped into a "family oriented" way of thinking. Perhaps a better way of thinking is to free yourself from families and develop a "surname oriented" filing system. I will attempt to walk you through the process of changing from a "family system" to a "surname system" for the care and preservation of your notes and documents.

To explain, let's forget about families for a moment. Let's assume that the genealogical events for individuals — which are found in the notes and documents — precede the work of filling in a family group sheet. And, if that is true, then the first papers that need to be organized are not the family sheets, but the notes and documents that are used to compile the family group sheets.

Organizing family group sheets, as you already know, is not the problem. The problem is finding that marriage record you know you have... you know when and where you found it the first time... you even remember the color of the walls of the library, the microfilm reader you were using, the people who were in the room at the time, and what you had for lunch that day — you just can't remember where you put that darn marriage record! I will propose a method that will allow you to find any marriage, any birth, any death, or any residence event for any person. And, you will be able to do it in seconds.

Problem Two: We gather genealogical information on more people than just our immediate ancestors.

As a person born with the name Dollarhide, I was born curious about where that name came from. Today, I collect any person I can find with the name, believing that we are probably related. Any genealogist with an unusual name in their background knows about this — we collect a lot of facts about a lot of unknown extra people simply because they have the right name.

Three Groups of People

Virtually everything we collect as genealogists can be associated with three groups of people. Therefore, the notes and documents that you have collected will have sheets of paper for:

1. **Ancestors.** Of course we are interested in our ancestors, and any piece of paper that gives the names of an ancestor is something we want to save, however slight.

2. **Collaterals.** These are people who are the brothers and sisters of our ancestors, plus their descendants. They are important to us because understanding their genealogy may lead to our own lineage. Therefore, we usually are interested in saving every instance where a known collateral's name is written down somewhere.

3. **Suspicious.** This may be the largest group of people we collect. We are always finding some person with the right name who lived in the right place and in the right time period. This means the person is highly suspicious of being an ancestor, or at least may be closely related. Because of the nature of genealogical research, these types of extra people cause us to collect much more paper than just for our ancestors. We don't want to lose contact with these people because they may turn out to be an ancestor, so we save every sheet of paper. Hence, our paper files grow and grow and grow.

Solving the Paper Collecting Problem

There is a solution to the paper collecting problem. Since we collect notes and documents for ancestors and collaterals, and because we add extra people with the same surname because we think they might be related, then why not create a well-organized database of information just for the notes and documents? Instead of saving notes and documents by family, we could save notes and documents by surname. Hey! That means you could save notes and documents on anyone! It also means you might be able to find a record when you want it.

More importantly, if you start thinking about "surnames" instead of "families" as the way you control the paper in your notes and documents file, you have some new options. For example, what if you treated the ancestors, collaterals, and suspicious people as equals? What effect would that have on your note taking? If you sorted your notes and documents by surnames instead of families, you could create a database of information that was not limited to a family relationship at all. Remember, the notes and documents are collected before a family group sheet is prepared. Therefore, a surname is a unifying factor which brings together people who are ancestors, collaterals, or suspects. It also frees you from a family-oriented filing system.

There is one other important unifying factor in genealogy, and that is the place where someone lived. For example, by collecting and then sorting all Dollarhides by whoever lived in North Carolina, regardless of their relationship to me, I would have a database of Dollarhide notes that would be fairly easy to organize. And, I would be able to create family group sheets from that database much easier. So, how do we go about creating a surname oriented database? We do it by following some simple rules.

Rules for Saving Notes and Documents

Let's forget that you still have this incredibly large pile of notes and documents sitting in the middle of your kitchen. Instead, let's assume that you are starting your genealogical research tomorrow. Everything is new. We will now start fresh. Under these conditions, I can give you some really good rules to follow and your genealogical collection will be the envy of every other genealogist you know because you will be able to find every event recorded for every person you have ever collected, every time, guaranteed. Here are my four rules:

1. Standardize the paper size
2. Separate sheets by surname
3. Separate surname sheets by the place of origin
4. Give every sheet a page number

Rule 1: Standardize the Paper Size

As students we learned how to prepare for a written essay in school. We were taught to use 3" x 5" index cards, noting such things as the author's name, publisher, date of publication, etc., followed by a brief quote or two from the source we had found in the library. This method worked well because the cards could be sorted easily and it provided a bibliography once the report had been written.

However, genealogists attempting to use this system will quickly discover that they rarely have enough room on the card to write all notes they may want to capture. Not only that, genealogists are fond of copying whole pages of text from books, not just a few notes here and there. To make matters worse, genealogists receive information from a variety of sources — letters from relatives, documents from vital statistics offices, interview notes, phone notes, or information from other genealogists. The nature of genealogical research does not allow the use of 3" x 5" cards effectively, because a separate collection of full-size documents would also be necessary.

We have also been known to go to the library without a note pad, using whatever paper we could beg, borrow, or steal, to write down the latest census data we found. If the little sheet of paper is covered with a larger sheet in the file box at home, the little sheet of paper will probably be in the "lost" category in the near future.

Standardizing the sheet size for taking notes using 8-1/2" x 11" paper solves this problem. If every note were taken on this sheet size, the smaller notes could be taped or pasted to standard size sheets to bring them into conformity; and if a researcher follows this simple rule faithfully, the ability to find notes and documents for later analysis will be enhanced.

To make this technique even better, using a pre-printed form to take all notes has several advantages. First, the sheet size will be controlled at the time the note is taken. 3-hole paper saves having to punch holes later, and the sheet has a place to be filed when taken home. An example of such a form for genealogical note-taking is the *Family Data Sheet*.

Rule 2: Separate Sheets by Surname

Genealogists can separate documents by the surname of the family to which they pertain. In other words, "Surname Books," that is, standard 3-hole notebooks, can be set up to hold the notes and documents which relate to one surname. One book would contain everything that is known about one surname, including those people who are ancestors, collaterals, or suspects.

At this level of collection it is not necessary to separate known ancestors from collaterals or suspicious persons. The important thing is that the person has the right surname and could be important to the project. As the notes are gathered, write the surname at the top of each page and devote an entire page to the notes for that surname or names connected with that surname. If a new surname of interest is encountered, start a new sheet for the new surname. This simple separation of notes by surname will allow you to file any sheet of paper logically and without having to recopy your notes when you get home.

Typically, genealogists find themselves sitting in front of a microfilm reader copying down notes from original records. Even if the genealogist was careful to copy all of the Johnson family records from one county, what happens sometimes is that another family surname pops up — something that was not expected. This happens frequently in the course of collecting genealogical records. The serious mistake is to mix these surnames on the same sheet of paper with another surname. If the Brown family is on the same sheet as the Johnson family, even though these two families were not related to each other, the only recourse later may be to use a pair of scissors to get the notes separated by the surname. Therefore, simply starting a new page when another surname is found will separate the surnames at the time the notes are first taken.

Separating documents into surname books limits what is stored in the books to just the notes and documents and does not admit such things as maps, lists of libraries, genealogical societies, or other material not directly related to a certain surname. (Remember there are two other categories. We're only talking about Notes and Documents right now.) The goal is to create a collection of reference material relating to a certain surname in such a way that family sheets can be prepared later — but with assurances that all of the known facts are easy to find.

A family record mentioning several different surnames that married into the family could all be saved as part of the main surname. The surname book contains information about the families and individuals important to the project, not necessarily just the known relatives. This is a key element in storing references in this manner. The problem of what to do with non-relatives has been solved: treat them the same as the relatives at this level of collection. If later research reveals that a reference item is not part of the family at all, the sheet can be removed and discarded. But, until then, the collection can contain any and all references to any surname of interest to the project.

Now the rules begin to make sense. If the same sheet size is used — 3-hole, 8-1/2" x 11" notepaper — and all surnames are separated on different sheets, a system of collecting notes and documents will pay off. With these two rules alone, the note does not need to be stacked on top of the pile at home — any new sheet can immediately go into a surname book as another page.

Rule 3: Separate Surname Sheets by the Place of Origin

Once the documents have been stored on the same sheet size and placed in the appropriate book for the surname, the next step is to break down the sheets by the place or origin of the record to be saved. The logic behind this concept needs to be explained.

There are three vital pieces of information every genealogist must know to pursue genealogical evidence: 1) a name, 2) a date, and 3) a place. With these three elements known, a treasure chest of information will be made available for further research. Of these three elements, the place is the one that tells you where to look for further information. The place of the event, such as the birthplace, place of death, place of marriage, place of residence, etc., is what a genealogist must know before a copy of that record can be obtained.

We live in a record-keeping society. The jurisdiction that created the record is the place. That jurisdiction must be known before we can find a record. If this fact is clear, then the idea of separating source material by the place is a logical step to take. Therefore, the many sheets of notes and documents pertaining to one surname can be further separated by the origin of the records. Experienced genealogists know that once the county of residence has been established, a treasure chest of information awaits there in the courthouse, the local library, a funeral home, a cemetery, a local genealogical society, etc., all of which can provide much important information about a family that lived in that locality. That information cannot be found without first knowing where to look.

Separating the sheets by the place is an easy task to control because virtually every single genealogical reference item will have a place attached to it. So, the top of the sheet should first show the surname for the record, followed by some designator for the place of origin.

For example, one surname book could contain all the Johnsons in Iowa in one section and Ohio Johnsons in another section. If the Johnson family of interest started out with an immigrant to New Jersey, followed by migrations later to Ohio, then Indiana, then Iowa, etc., these states could be arranged in that particular order — which would tend to put the family reference material in loose chronological order for the time periods they were in a particular state. This method of collecting source material will place records for certain individuals in more than one place section if a person moved from state to state over the course of his life. Don't worry about this yet — we are going to get all of these place-oriented records back when we create family group sheets — so, get the surnames together in one book, then divide the book by the places of the records.

The place designator can be broken down further. If there were many Johnsons in Ohio, it may be worthwhile to separate this section by county. The important thing about this method of organizing notes and documents is that when information about the Johnson family in Ohio is needed, a genealogist knows where to look for what is known about the family in that area. It is also the logical place to file a new piece of information.

The *Family Data Sheet* example indicates how a surname/place designator can be used, indicated at the top right-hand corner of the form. A two-letter code commonly used by the U.S. Postal Service is an effective way of giving a place designation. When the note or document is first being prepared, write the surname at the top of the page, followed by the place designator. The pre-printed form, of course, gives a genealogist a reminder of what needs to be done for every note and document.

Rule 4: Give Every Sheet a Page Number

The fourth rule is to simply give every page in the surname book a number. With the surname notebooks organized in sections for the places, each sheet can be given a number that allows for the retrieval and return of sheets to a proper position. A sheet number need only be a consecutive number starting with 1, adding numbers as sheets are accumulated.

A full sheet number might be Johnson/OH/24, meaning the sheet belongs in the Johnson surname book in the Ohio section, and within that section it is page 24. This sheet number is assigned on a "first come — first served" basis, so there is no need to re-arrange sheets later to get 1790 records before 1870 records. Genealogists find and collect records in random order, so they can be filed randomly too. This allows for adding sheets within a section as the records are found.

But, since the references have already been sorted by surname/place, the sheet number is simply a designator to put a sheet back into a known position; and it provides the means of indexing reference sheets later. The page number is a key element in this filing system. If an index is to be prepared in the future, or if a genealogist plans to use a computer some day, page numbers will be critically important.

Back to the Pile of Paper

Now that we have reviewed the four rules for taking new notes and setting up surname books, what about the mess you still have lying in the middle of your kitchen floor? Well, you will need the following items before you can get started:

- A good pair of scissors

- A bottle of Elmer's glue (or some other kind of stick-um), or Scotch tape (or Irish tape, which doesn't have to be returned to its owner after you use it.)

- A felt marker (color optional)

- A three-hole punch

- Several cardboard boxes, one for each surname you have

- Several 3-ring binders, at least one for each surname you have

- Set of sheet dividers for each binder

- 8-1/2" x 11" blank white paper (one ream should do it)

- Knee pads

- A sign that warns your family, "fines are double in work areas"

Start slow. Pick up a piece of paper from the pile. What surname does it relate to? Smith? Write "Smith" at the top of the page. What place does it relate to? Kansas? Write "KS" after Smith. Get a box and mark it "Smith". Place the first sheet of paper in the Smith box. Now get another sheet of paper from the pile and do the same thing. New Surname? Get another box.

Along about the third piece of paper, you will probably discover that both Smith and Johnson are mentioned on that one. If these two names did not marry each other or have some special connection, then you need to use your scissors and cut the Smith portion apart from the Johnson portion. Now get two blank 8-1/2" x 11" sheets of paper. Stick or tape the Johnson note on one sheet and the Smith note on the other. Label the top of each sheet with the surname and place. Put them in a cardboard box for each surname.

You will also discover some sheets early on that do not lend themselves to be cut up. These are the ones that mention several different surnames in the same paragraph. Cutting up these type of sheets won't work well, so put these to one side so you can take them to the nearest photocopy machine. You will need to make as many copies as there are ancestral surnames mentioned. Remember, we are trying to separate all of our notes and documents by surname — if that means copying a resource more than once, that is what it will take.

A marriage record is an example of two surnames mentioned that properly should go in two different surname books. You could make a copy of the marriage record so one could be filed with the groom's surname, the other with the bride's maiden surname… or you could simply make a quick note on a new sheet with the names, dates, places, and a cross-reference note that tells a reader that a full marriage document is filed in a different surname book. That cross-reference note is a full size sheet and could take the place of another marriage document in another surname book.

As you see the sheets building up in the boxes, you should begin to see what is happening. You are building surname files, and isn't it exciting! But even if you are not bubbling with excitement yet, this is what you will need to do to your current notes and documents to adopt this system. If you are willing to do it, you will love what happens when you have them all prepared this way.

Once you have all the sheets of paper off the floor, your pile will not exist anymore. You now have several cardboard boxes with nifty stacks of 8-1/2" x 11" paper in them. So, grab the box of your choice (how about Johnson) and get a 3-ring binder that will hold all of them. Too many for one binder? Add more binders as necessary. Next, get someone to clean off the kitchen table. Now, go through the entire Johnson stack and make smaller stacks of the Johnson sheets for each place the Johnsons lived. Sheets that are not already 3-hole punched need to be punched now.

Creating stacks for each place is sort of like correlating pages, and you could possibly involve other members of your family in this exercise. "OK, Don, I want you to collect all of the Johnsons in Iowa in your stack. And, Angie, you have Ohio." If the family starts fighting over which state they get, promise that when they are done they will all get fed. (Which, of course, is something that none of the family had done together since you first got into genealogy.)

If you have sheets that are smaller than 8-1/2" x 11," then stick or tape them to a full size sheet and add the surname and place at the top of the page. If you have documents that are larger, you can fold them so they will go into a notebook, or you can make or buy a "pocket" sheet. These can be purchased from a K-Mart, Wal-Mart, or perhaps in the school supplies area of a local supermarket. The purchased pocket sheets are pre-punched for 3-holes and have a pocket where an over-sized folded document can be inserted.

If your pile includes original documents, you may want to make photocopies of them, which would also allow for reducing the size, if necessary, to fit your notebooks. You can treat original photographs the same way — make copies for the notebooks. The originals can then be stored with other documents or photos in a container kept in a dry place. (A good selection of acid-neutral storage boxes for extended safe storage of original documents and photographs is identified in Heritage Quest's catalog.)

Once you have gone through one surname and separated the sheets by place, each sheet in a surname/place stack can now be numbered. You can arrange these sheets any way you want at this time, but any new sheets will be added at the back with continued numbering. If the first stack you take on is the Johnson/Iowa stack, start numbering the sheets IA-1, IA-2, IA-3, and so on. Do the same for each stack of sheets for each place you have separated. When this is done you can place all of the sheets in a 3-ring binder. Use the sheet dividers to separate the sheets by states/places.

Any expression of wild and crazy celebration at this point is perfectly in order. You are permitted to take your shoes off, let your hair down, shout with glee, or hug and kiss any person who happens to be in the room. You are finished with the pile!

Retrieving Notes and Compiling Family Sheets

If all of the notes and documents are organized as described above, a genealogist has the means of locating multiple sheets for analysis. The process of comparing information from the notes is one which most experienced genealogists understand. However, the problem of locating every research item can be frustrating if the notes are not in a place where they can be removed (or returned) easily.

The next step of compiling a family sheet is the point where most genealogists compare the notes, evaluate the contradictions that always occur, and then make a decision about the dates, places, and events necessary to enter information about the family members. This process is sometimes lengthy and worrisome and often leads to ideas where new research might be necessary. With a large collection of research notes, the process is even more complicated; and some means of indexing the information becomes critical.

With notes and documents easily retrieved from the surname notebooks, a family sheet can be prepared more easily; but more importantly, a complete list of every sheet that was used to compile the family information can be cited.

The Importance of Genealogical Evidence

Genealogists have at their disposal a rule of law called "the preponderance of evidence." It is possible — if one can fully document all sources — to make assertions about the relationships between people. There may not be a single document that states, "he was the son of..." in your document files; but there may be overwhelming evidence to demonstrate that a relationship of father to son was indeed the case. If a court of law in the U.S. can accept such evidence, then it can be used by genealogists as well.

In fact, there are numerous instances in which professional genealogists have testified in court about genealogical evidence regarding an heir to property or some matter in which genealogical evidence was in question. Genealogical evidence is no different than the evidence provided in a criminal case, where the prosecuting attorney must produce evidence that the accused was indeed the criminal. However, the important fact about evidence is that everyone who reviews it must come to the same conclusion. Therefore, the pieces of evidence must be made available so that anyone can scrutinize the findings. If the same conclusion is reached, then it is indeed possible to make an assertion about "the son of..." without having a single document that actually states that fact.

Any references, however slight, should be in the notes and documents collection. This means, for instance, that an obituary should be obtained even if the death certificate for this person has already been acquired. It also means that any other piece of evidence relating to that death should be gathered, e.g., survivors' memories, funeral programs, cemetery office records, tombstone inscriptions, stone mason records, insurance papers, social security records, and anything that may give clues about the survivors of the deceased. The more references collected, the more information that will be revealed about the ancestors or descendants of the person who died. Adding multiple references to a death or other event is the way we build a preponderance of evidence. This is the method in which a genealogist can prove something without a shadow of doubt being cast on the evidence. A complete list of references should accompany every genealogical presentation, whether the presentation is a few family group sheets or a thousand-page book.

Preparing a List for a Family Sheet

There are several ways of listing the sources and itemizing the evidence for genealogical purposes. First, a genealogist could simply write a narrative which describes the steps taken, listing every source and the conclusions reached. Second, a formal list could be prepared that itemizes all sources that make any mention of one person. And third, such a list could be prepared for each family group showing the page number in the notes/documents collection where the information is found.

This latter method has merit if the family sheet is being prepared anyway, so why not simply list every reference that was used to compile the family information? Better yet, why not use the back side of the family sheet to do it? This is good record-keeping because in compiling the family sheet, every reference item from the documents file can be listed one at a time. Then, as new information is added, the new reference item can be added to the list as well.

Remember the suggestion was for every reference sheet to have a number — now the importance of that page number is evident. But, beyond the simple reference to the page, more information might be worthwhile having in the list. An example of how this system can be implemented is a family sheet designed to list the references. The sample of a *Compiled Family Data Sheet* demonstrates how this method works. The front of the sheet is a standard group sheet for a family, giving the husband, wife, and children, with their pertinent genealogical data. The back side of the sheet has a place to list every *Reference Family Data Sheet* that was used for that particular family.

Note that the first thing needed is to tell the genealogist which surname book the item came from, what section within the surname book, and what page number within that section. "Dollarhide/IN/3" indicates that the reference is in the Dollarhide surname book in the Indiana section, and within that section, it is page 3.

There are advantages in listing all references on the family sheet in this way. Not only does the list indicate every research item that was used to compile the family group, it provides a list that can be mailed to other genealogists showing what has been collected for that family. Genealogists who receive letters from other genealogists asking "everything you have on the Brown family" can send the list of references first.

The list also tells a genealogist where to find records that may be stored in more than one place. For example, records concerning Nancy Pierson before her marriage can be stored with the Pierson surname book. Records after her marriage to Jesse Dollarhide can be stored in the Dollarhide surname book.

A copy need not be made for each book if the list indicates where each particular reference has been filed.

List References for One Person

Another optional step in compiling information is to make a sheet for each pedigree ancestor. A special form to do this — a *Master Data Sheet* — is shown for Mary Winslow. The concept of having one sheet for all of the vital statistics for one person is one which many genealogists find useful. This particular form has expanded the information about one person and includes a small pedigree chart to assign an ID number to each pedigree ancestor. (ID numbers are discussed in detail in "*Essay 5, Genealogical Numbering Systems.*")

On the back side of the *Master Data Sheet* is another form called a Research Log. This lists every *Reference Family Data Sheet* that mentions Mary Winslow. It is a similar listing to the one on the *Compiled Family Data Sheet*, and may repeat some of the same information. The advantage of this is that it enables you to locate each item for one person and then prepare the master vital statistics for that person. The individual list can be made for any person, not just for ancestors.

With a well organized Notes and Documents file, particularly one with page numbers for every sheet of paper, you have several other options to create an index to the names appearing in it. We described one method of using the back of a family group sheet to show a list of references, giving the name of the surname book, place section, and page number where the full details are stored. The same sort of list can be prepared for individuals using a *Master Data Sheet/Research Log* form that allows for listing every reference for one person.

An index of the names in your Notes and Document paper database could also be prepared using 3" x 5" index cards, a Rolodex file, or using a computer database program. The fact that your notes and documents are well organized will give you several options to prepare an index if listing the sources on family sheets or individual sheets does not cover everyone in your paper database.

Finally, you can organize your genealogical notes and documents, but only if you are willing to separate them from other types of paper in your files, such as compiled sheets and research aids. With a well organized set of notes and documents, and with page numbers assigned to each sheet of paper, you can make lists on family sheets or individual sheets that will give you access to your notes in seconds. In addition, you will have the means of preparing more sophisticated indexes to your notes by using computer database programs.

For more detailed information about the organizational system described in this essay, see *Managing A Genealogical Project* (Baltimore: Genealogical Publishing Co., Inc., 1988, rev. 1991, rev. 1999) by William Dollarhide. The *Managing* book describes the same rules for organizing notes and documents and has chapters on pedigree numbering, descendancy numbering, a numbering scheme which combines both ancestors and descendants, creating computer databases, reviews of several genealogical software products, and presentation techniques for publishing a genealogical work.

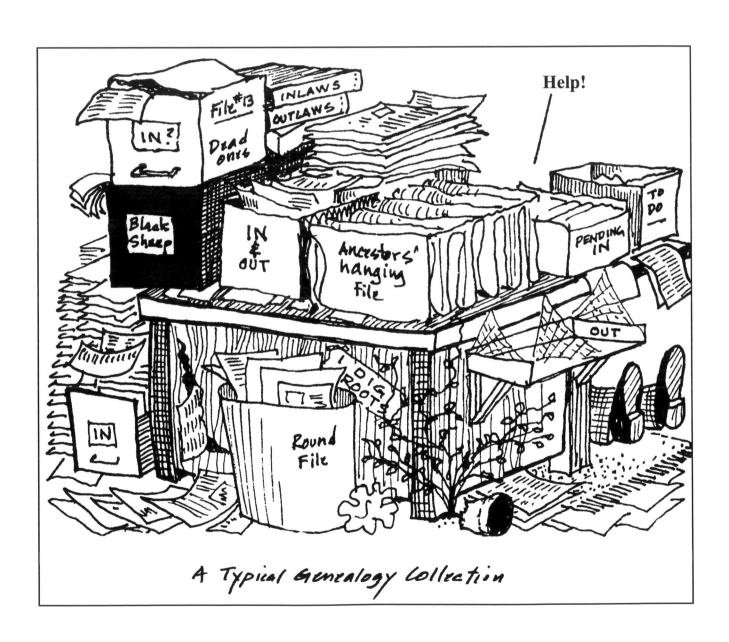

A Typical Genealogy Collection

Genealogical Numbering Systems

Pedigree/Ahnentafel Numbering

The German word "ahnentafel" translates to "ancestor table" in English. The German word is pronounced AW-NEN-TAWFULL. An ahnentafel is truly awful. (In the sense that it is awe inspiring — not awfully bad). Ahnentafel is the German word for pedigree. To Americans, a pedigree is an identification of a person's direct ancestors. An American pedigree can be expressed as a diagram showing the ancestors of a person, starting with a first person, usually a person alive today, and moves back in time to that person's parents, grandparents, great-grandparents, and so on.

The English have a broader definition of the word "pedigree" which can be the same as what we Americans would call a "descendancy." The English began using the word pedigree back during the time of an influential French-speaking visitor named William the Conqueror. In French, the word pedigree means "the foot of the goose," because, apparently, a goose's foot resembles the branches of tree.

Dating back to the time of Kaiser Wilhelm I, the Germans invented a numbering scheme for a pedigree in which unique ID numbers were assigned to each person in an ancestor table. Unlike an American pedigree diagram, where numbers for people keep changing when you run out of paper on a chart and repeat a person on another chart, the ahnentafel numbering system continues the numbers in a very logical, and typically German, scheme.

But, the difference between an American pedigree and a German ahnentafel is only a matter of how to assign ID numbers to ancestors. The ahnentafel system not only allows for unique ID numbers for every ancestor in a pedigree, it allows for different methods of displaying or publishing a pedigree. And, since the Germans are known for their keen sense of logic and order, using an ahnentafel system has some advantages over an American pedigree numbering scheme.

Americans have always been borrowers, and the German ahnentafel system has been borrowed by many American genealogists, particularly those who want to copy the German's penchant for efficiency, logic, and order.

A Typical American Pedigree Chart

A typical American pedigree chart usually has room for four generations. Starting on the first chart with number 1, the father of that person is number 2, the mother number 3. The grandparents are numbers 4, 5, 6, and 7, and the great-grandparents are numbers 8 through 15:

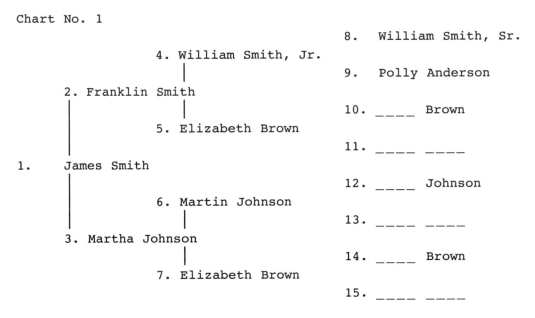

```
Chart No. 1
                                              8.   William Smith, Sr.
                     4. William Smith, Jr.
                        |                     9.   Polly Anderson
      2. Franklin Smith
         |              |                     10. ____  Brown
                        5. Elizabeth Brown
         |                                    11. ____  ____
  1.    James Smith
         |                                    12. ____  Johnson
                     6. Martin Johnson
         |              |                     13. ____  ____
      3. Martha Johnson
         |                                    14. ____  Brown
                     7. Elizabeth Brown
                                              15. ____  ____
```

On the first chart of four generations, there are some simple rules that can be seen for each of the numbered positions of ancestors:

1. Except for the first person, all husbands/males in the diagram are shown above their wives/females.

2. Except for the first person, who can be male or female, all males/husbands have an ID number which is an even number.

3. All females/wives have an ID number which is an odd number, a number one higher than their husband's number.

4. The ID number of the father of any person is double that person's number. Therefore, the father of number 1 is number 2. The father of number 3 is number 6. The father of number 6 is number 12, and so on.

5. The ID number of the mother of any person is double that person's number plus one. Thus, the mother of number 5 is 10 + 1, or number 11.

All of these rules apply to the first chart. If another pedigree chart is needed to continue the ancestry, a cross-reference is necessary because the numbers start over again with number 1 for the first person on the chart:

Chart No. 2
No. 1 on this chart is the same
as No. 8 on chart No. 1.

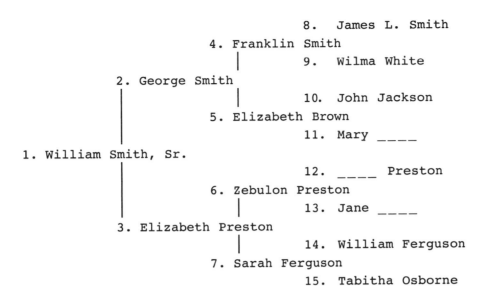

```
                                    8.   James L. Smith
                      4. Franklin Smith
                         |          9.   Wilma White
           2. George Smith
              |          |          10.  John Jackson
              |       5. Elizabeth Brown
              |          |          11.  Mary ____
1. William Smith, Sr.
              |                     12.  ____ Preston
              |       6. Zebulon Preston
              |          |          13.  Jane ____
           3. Elizabeth Preston
                         |          14.  William Ferguson
                      7. Sarah Ferguson
                                    15.  Tabitha Osborne
```

Here's the situation. On chart #2, the first person is back to being person No. 1. All of the rules about doubling to find a father or mother that made sense on the first chart are used over again for each new chart. In addition, a cross-reference note is needed somewhere on chart #2 that states, "Person No. 1 on chart No. 2 is the same as Person No. 8 on chart No. 1."

If person No. 1 on chart No. 2 used to have the ID number 8 on chart No. 1, that means that a genealogist is forced to keep track of charts in addition to keeping track of people. When going from chart No. 1 to chart No. 2, the use of unique ID numbers has been lost because the ID numbers have changed.

Ahnentafel vs Pedigree Numbering

Essentially, to refer to a pedigree as an ahnentafel, a genealogist needs to modify the numbers so that every ancestor keeps a unique ID number that never changes. Here's the effect of an ahnentafel on a new chart No. 2 using the German Numbering System:

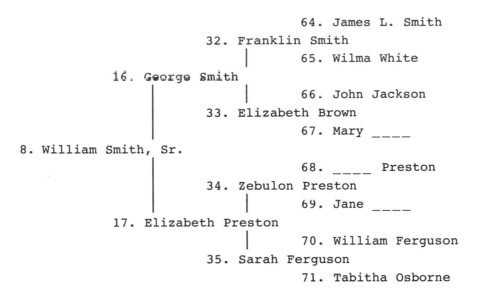

```
                                        64. James L. Smith
                          32. Franklin Smith
                              |           65. Wilma White
            16. George Smith
                |             |           66. John Jackson
                |         33. Elizabeth Brown
                |                         67. Mary ____
    8. William Smith, Sr.
                |                         68. ____ Preston
                |         34. Zebulon Preston
                |             |           69. Jane ____
            17. Elizabeth Preston
                              |           70. William Ferguson
                          35. Sarah Ferguson
                                        71. Tabitha Osborne
```

The ancestor who was ID no. 8 on chart No. 1 is repeated as ID no. 8 on chart no. 2. It's as simple as that. Why change ID numbers?

Now the same rules apply on any new chart. The father of No. 8 is No. 16. The father of No. 16 is No. 32, and so on. The rule for adding 1 to a male's ID number for each female follows as well.

In fact, the main difference is that ID numbers continue to rise. Regardless of what chart on which a person appears, an ID number never changes. As a result, the ID numbers are unique and can be used for other presentations of a pedigree not possible without them.

In addition, ahnentafel charts can be numbered to indicate the ID number of the person who starts the chart. If No. 1 starts chart No. 1, why can't the chart starting with ID No. 8 be the starting person on Chart No. 8? With this concept, a chart can be started with any person in the first position; and that person's ID number can also identify the chart number.

Ahnentafel Lists

A list of your direct ancestors can be prepared in numerical order. All the rules from the pedigree still work, i.e., to find the father of any person, double that person's number; and to find a mother of any person, double the person's number and add one.

1. James Smith
2. Franklin Smith
3. Martha Johnson
4. William Smith, Jr.
5. Elizabeth Brown
6. Martin Johnson
7. Mary Black
8. William Smith, Sr.

9. Polly Anderson
10. _____ Brown
11. _____ _____
12. _____ Johnson
13. _____ _____
14. _____ Black
15. _____ _____
16. George Smith
17. Elizabeth Preston
18. James Anderson
19. Martha Ann Pool
...and so on...

The ahnentafel list above is no different than a pedigree diagram, but the ancestors are listed in a table. Note that in this list certain names were added where the surname could be predicted. For example, the father of any male can be predicted to have the same surname. Therefore, it was possible to predict that number 10 would be a Brown, as was the case also for number 12, Johnson, and number 14, Black.

Surname List

The simplicity of the ahnentafel is what makes it so practical. For example, the rule about all males having even numbers and all females having odd numbers gives a genealogist another list that can be very useful — a surname list.

Since every female ancestor has a different surname, listing females in numerical order presents a list of every different surname which appears in a pedigree:

1. Smith, James
3. Johnson, Martha
5. Brown, Elizabeth
7. Black, Mary
9. Anderson, Polly
...and so on...

If the above list were continued — being all odd numbers — it would list every female in the pedigree. (Remember that number one is the only odd number that can be male or female). But, the list is also a listing of every *different* surname in the entire pedigree.

A genealogist who has identified more than thirty different surnames is engaged in a very large pedigree project. Counting surnames is another way of judging the size of a pedigree. The surname list is possible without using ahnentafel numbers, of course, but the numbers add an element of priority. The lower the number, the closer to the starting person in the pedigree. Therefore, a surname list can act as a list of names in their numerical order, but also in their order of priority or importance back in time. (A rule that tells you where you should be working on your pedigree, is to work on those surnames with unanswered questions and which are closer to No. 1 in numerical order).

Ancestor Table

Behind each of the odd numbers in a surname list is a line of males with the same surname. So, an arrangement of the ahnentafel allows another method of viewing a lineage from a pedigree chart — this time just for one surname. I'll call this type of list an "ancestor table."

Compile an ancestor table by starting with any odd number, then double that number to find the father of that person, double again to continue, such as shown in the list below:

>   3. Martha Johnson
>   6. Martin Johnson
> 12. Samuel Johnson
> 24. William Johnson
> 48. Henry Johnson
> 96. Henry Johnson
> 192. Henry Johnson
> …and so on…

The same list could be prepared showing all of the spouses of the Johnson men. An ancestor table can be prepared for each surname, one page for one lineage of the same name, creating a series of sheets that can store the names, spouses, dates, and places for each genealogical event, e.g., birth, marriage, or death.

Ahnentafel numbers lend themselves to more options for displaying ancestors.

Numbering Family Sheets

For every pair of ancestors on a pedigree chart or ancestor table, a family group sheet needs to be prepared. A rule in genealogy is to treat the brothers and sisters of our ancestors as equals — that is, we need to gather sources and records about the siblings just like they were direct ancestors. (By coincidence, the siblings have the same set of parents as your ancestors.)

Genealogists learn that the place where a family lived is critical information in locating sources today. In some cases, it may be necessary to identify siblings, their spouses, their children, their grandchildren, or more… and, hopefully, locate a relative alive today who can share information about your common ancestor.

The ID numbers for each ancestor can be used for identifying the position of a particular family group sheet in numerical order. For example, the first group sheet in a notebook might be for number two and number three (the father and mother of number 1). The first family group sheet can be identified as "2/3" indicating the father/mother ID numbers, followed by groups sheets for each pair from a pedigree chart:

  2/3 (father is 2, mother is 3)
  4/5 (father is 4, mother is 5)
  6/7 (father is 6, mother is 7)
  8/9 (father is 8, mother is 9)
10/11 (father is 10, mother 11)
12/13 (father is 12, mother is 13)
14/15 (father is 14, mother is 15)
…and so on…

With this arrangement, the ID numbers identify the pedigree position of each family sheet. The sheets can be organized in a notebook numerically rather than alphabetically by surname. (The fact that several families all have a surname that starts with "B" may place ancestral and collateral families together who are not related at all.)

But, the real advantage to organizing family sheets in numerical order is when there are many "extra" families. A family group sheet becomes a tremendous tool in understanding the places where an ancestor and each sibling was born, married, or died. It is necessary to have more choices for research on the parents by drawing from information about each of the siblings. If you need to branch out to the collateral siblings of your ancestors, then an ID number for these extra people will be useful.

ID Numbers for Collaterals

Your ancestor's brothers and sisters along with their descendants are *collateral* to the pedigree. There is a method of giving all these related persons ID numbers as well.

But first… let's modify the ahnentafel numbering rules slightly. What if we assigned ID numbers to all our ancestors with a number that adds a decimal and a zero, such as:

  1 = 1.0
  2 = 2.0
  3 = 3.0
  4 = 4.0
  5 = 5.0
  …and so on…

An ID number adding the "point zero" will be reserved for indicating a direct ancestor.

Now you can give ID numbers to the brothers and sisters of 1.0 as 1.1, 1.2, 1.3, or to the brothers and sisters of 2.0 as 2.1, 2.2, 2.3, and so on.

If you prepare a family group sheet for your ancestor number 12 and 13 (now to be shown as 12.0 and 13.0), their children could be numbered 6.1, 6.2, 6.3, and so on. The decimal order can indicate an approximate birth order for all siblings except for the sibling who is your ancestor.

Since we are reserving ID 6.0 for ancestor number six (6 and 6.0 are identical), it becomes a flag that indicates which of the siblings is the direct ancestor. But, the birth order for the ancestor needs to be determined by his/her position on a family group listing.

Let's say ancestor 12.0 and 13.0 had four children and your ancestor was the fourth child. That child would be ID number 6.0 who is one-half the number of his father 12.0 — remember the rule of doubling to find a father, this is going in the other direction — so divide in half any father's ID number to find the ID number of "pedigree child," for example:

> 12.0 Father
> 13.0 Mother
>> 6.1 child 1 (male or female)
>> 6.2 child 2 (male or female)
>> 6.3 child 3 (male or female)
>> 6.0 child 4 (your ancestor, a male)

What if 12.0 and 13.0 had four children and your ancestor was the second child in the family:

> 12.0 Father
> 13.0 Mother
>> 6.1 child 1 (male or female)
>> 6.0 child 2 (Your ancestor, a male)
>> 6.3 child 3 (male or female)
>> 6.4 child 4 (male or female)

In the example above, your ancestor retains the number 6.0 regardless of his position in the birth order of siblings. There is no 6.2 because 6.0 takes that position as the second child.

The rule of odd and even for direct ancestors is maintained by adding "point zero" to each ancestor's ID number. However, for brothers or sisters of an ancestor, the ID number mush apply to either male or female — therefore, 6.3 simply indicates that that person is a (male or female) collateral sibling of your (male) ancestor 6.0.

On some family sheets the order of children must be approximated due to a lack of precise dates of birth from reference sources. In some cases, genealogists list the children in the only way possible — by guessing. If exact dates of birth are not known, the same would be true for assigning ID numbers to the siblings of an ancestor. But, once the numbers are assigned, you should not change them... because we can use the collateral ID numbers to identify the *descendants* of siblings as well.

Around the Brick Wall

Every genealogist will eventually hit a "brick wall" on a particular lineage. This occurs when information about the parents of a person is seemingly impossible to locate. There is only one way of dealing with an impassable brick wall, and that is to go another direction using the *collateral* lines to solve the problem.

For example, a female ancestor who died in childbirth at the age of sixteen may have left very few marks to follow. Or, a young man killed in battle may have had a wife and child, but never owned land, never left any documents to find in local records, and never appeared in any history books. These are "brick walls."

But each of these ancestors may have had brothers or sisters who lived to a ripe old age, left many documents, family Bibles, memories, etc.; and these people are the ones a genealogist must trace to solve the brick wall problems.

Identifying the collateral lines that connect with a pedigree — and then tracing the descendants of those collateral lines — can become unmanageable unless there is a numbering system that integrates both the ahnentafel (pedigree) numbers with a descendancy numbering system. One could think of the pedigree as moving "up" and the descendancy moving "down." The brick wall in the pedigree causes us to move sideways (to a sibling), then down again.

Assigning ID numbers to ancestors then joining numbers for collaterals will allow a method of organizing, sorting, and finding related families.

Here is a method of assigning ID numbers to a collateral family based on their numerical relationship to an ahnentafel/pedigree:

> 12   John Smith, Sr. (father) (pedigree ancestor)
> 13   Elizabeth Jones (mother) (pedigree ancestor)
> 6.1   John Smith, Jr. (1st child), m 6.1*, Martha Black
> 6.0   William Smith (2nd child), (pedigree child), m 7.0, Jane Doe
> 6.3   Wilma Smith, (3rd child), married 6.3*, James Brown

Collateral family:

> 6.1   John Smith, Jr.
> 6.1*   Martha Black
> 6.11   John Smith, III (1st child) married, 6.11*, Karen Jackson
> 6.12   Evelyn Smith, (2nd child), married 6.12*, Harold Johnson

Spouses can be assigned numbers that are derived from the collateral, e.g., the spouse of 6.1 is 6.1*. Children of 6.1 and 6.1* can continue the numbers (6.11, 6.12, etc.) of the collateral sibling by adding a digit and birth order.

ID Numbers for Collateral Descendants

Once we have established ID numbers for our ancestors and collateral siblings of ancestors, the next step is to control the children of collateral siblings. Using an earlier example of 12.0 who married 13.0, their child was 6.0. The rule to find the ID number for a father of any person in a pedigree is to double that person's number. In this case, go the other direction to find the "pedigree child" of any father by dividing the father's number in half.

Say that ancestor 6.0 died young. We know the ID numbers for his parents (12.0 and 13.0) but we do not know all of the details we need to know about them. In this case, it may be necessary to identify the descendants of 6.0's brothers and sisters, with the goal of finding a person alive today who may share information. To do this, we need to assign ID numbers to all spouses, children, and all known descendants of the siblings of ancestor 6.0. It may be necessary to identify these descendants for several generations; and if so, there should be a numbering scheme that will handle it without causing confusion.

Typically, we find enough information from our research to put a family together. The information may come from census records, family Bible records, family memories, or a myriad of other sources. We can then create a family group sheet with the known information and ID numbers for each member of the family, such as the example below:

> 12.0   Henry Johnson
> 13.0   Martha (– – – – –)
>   6.1   Elizabeth Johnson
>   6.2   William Johnson
>   6.3   Mary Johnson
>   6.0   John Johnson

John Johnson (6.0) is our ancestor, as is Henry Johnson (12.0) and Martha (– – – – –) (13.0). We need to know the maiden name for John's mother, plus more information about the parents.

But, if John Johnson died as a young man, leaving little information to trace, we need to conduct research and add more information about

John's siblings. For example, we may discover more information about John's brother — and we will need to prepare a family group sheet and show the brother's wife and children along with their ID numbers:

> 6.2   William Johnson (brother of 6.0)
> 6.2*   Wilma (– – – – –) (spouse of 6.2)
>   6.21   Sarah Johnson
>   6.22   James Johnson
>   6.23   Samuel Johnson

To assign an ID number to William Johnson's wife, we added an asterisk (*), meaning *spouse of 6.2*. (Had William Johnson married more than once, we could identify his spouses with 6.2*1 and 6.2*2 to indicate "spouse 1" and "spouse 2.")

The children of William Johnson use his number, but add a digit to show their birth order. The next generation need not have another decimal, just an added number such as 6.21, 6.22, 6.23, and so on.

Using this method, we can continue to assign collateral ID numbers to any number of generations, for example, to the children of 6.21 (Sarah Johnson), a child of 6.2. But, let's say that Sarah was married twice and had children with both husbands. Numbers for her first family would be:

6.21*1   Robert Jones, Sr. (spouse of 6.21)
6.21   Sarah Johnson (daughter of 6.2, niece of 6.0)
   6.211   Robert Jones, Jr.
   6.212   Elizabeth Jones

And, her second family would be:

6.21*2   Henry Wadsworth
6.21   Sarah (Johnson) Jones
   6.213   William Wadsworth
   6.214   John Wadsworth
   6.215   Mary Wadsworth

On separate family sheets, both of the above families can be identified. Sarah Johnson is the collateral descendant, so her number (6.21) is used to continue the descendancy. Though she married twice and had children with both husbands, the numbers for her children can still be in consecutive order: 6.211, 6.212, 6.213, 6.214, and 6.215, because she was the mother of five children.

The collateral ID numbers will work for either a male or a female. Adding the asterisk (*) is simply an indication of a person who married a collateral descendant. Her first spouse was Robert Jones, Sr. (6.21*1) and her second spouse was Henry Wadsworth (6.21*2), both of whom have numbers based on her number.

What ties all of these collateral people to the person who is number one on a pedigree? They are all connected to number 6.0, an ancestor.

Who are the common ancestors shared by these collaterals and the person who is number one? The parents of number 6.0. The father of 6.0 can be determined to be number 12.0 by doubling number 6.0, the mother by adding one, or number 13.0.

More Than Nine Children?

Note that the numbers to the right of the decimal are for a descendancy, and each single digit represents a generational step. So, a two-digit number for one generation is not allowed — if there were more than nine children in a family, a 10th child will cause these numbers to go awry. Therefore, to show a family with ten or more children, use this method:

> 6.23   Samuel Johnson
> 6.23*   Sarah Flint
>   6.231   William Johnson
>   6.232   John Johnson
>   6.233   Mary Johnson
>   6.234   Henry Johnson
>   6.235   Frank Johnson
>   6.236   Elizabeth Johnson
>   6.237   Wilma Johnson
>   6.238   Martha Johnson
>   6.239   Jemima Johnson
>   6.23A   Polly Johnson (10th child of 6.23)
>   6.23B   Margaret Johnson (11th child 6.23)
>   6.23C   Walter Johnson (12th child of 6.23)

The numbers for the 10th, 11th, 12th or more children should be represented with a single character — a letter "A" equals 10, a letter "B" equals 11, and so on. Now you can identify larger family groups and maintain a single digit for each person/generation. After child number 9, all 26 letters of the alphabet are available, for a combined total of 35 sibling positions. (This may look like the Hexadecimal numbering system, but it is not. The hexadecimal is base 16 rather than base 10, but the numbers A, B, C, etc., do not have the same positions as in the example shown above.)

Continuing a collateral family with Walter Johnson (6.21C) as the father would appear as shown below:

> 6.23C   Walter Johnson
> 6.23C*1   Elizabeth Brown
>   6.23C1   William Johnson
>   6.23C2   Penny Johnson
>   6.23C3   Helen Johnson
>   6.23C4   Allen Johnson

The numbers to the right of the decimal represent a descendancy. You could think of the pedigree starting with number one as going "up." In this case, we went up to 6.0, then sideways to a sibling, 6.2, then "down" (in a descendancy) to 6.23, 6.23C, and then 6.23C1, and so on.

For the ID number 6.23C1, the numbers can be read as "the 1st child, of the 10th child, of the 3rd child, of the 2nd child of ancestor number 12.0."

Parents or Siblings of a Spouse

It may be necessary to identify parents or siblings of a spouse who join the collateral descendancy. In any pedigree, the parents of the first person (ID 1.0) are ID 2.0 and ID 3.0. To assign a number to the parents of Elizabeth Brown (6.21C*1) above, a signal needs to be used to show that a descendancy is ending and a pedigree is beginning:

Parents of Elizabeth Brown, ID 6.21C*1

> 6.21C*1:2   Mortimer Brown (father)
> 6.21C*1:3   Mariana Black (mother)

In the above examples, the signal that a descendancy is ending and an ahnentafel is starting is the colon (:). This is a way of giving an ID number to the parents of Elizabeth Brown (shown as either 6.21C*1 or 6.21C*1.0). If Elizabeth were ID number 1.0 in an ahnentafel, her parents would be ID 2.0 and ID 3.0.

And, if the siblings of Elizabeth Brown need to be identified, show them as follows:

> 6.21C* 1.1   sibling
> 6.21C* 1.2   sibling
>   6.21C* 1.0   Elizabeth Brown
>   6.21C* 1.4   sibling

Brothers and sisters of Elizabeth Brown can also be assigned ID numbers if a family sheet needs to be prepared — or if you just want a number for these extra people for sorting purposes. In such cases, just add "point-zero" to a spouse's ID number; then the siblings can be assigned numbers as shown above.

Previous or Later Marriages For an Ancestor

Another situation that needs to be considered is the assignment of ID numbers for children from a previous or later marriage for an ancestor. For example, if your ancestor, number 12.0, were previously married, the first spouse needs to have a number based on his number.

Ancestor 12.0 with first wife:

> 12.0   Henry Johnson
> 12.0*1   Margaret Perry
>   6.1   Elizabeth Johnson
>   6.2   William Johnson

Numbering for the pedigree family, ancestor 12.0 with ancestor 13.0, his second wife is:

> 12.0   Henry Johnson
> 13.0   Martha (– – – – –)
>   6.3   Mary Johnson
>   6.0   John Johnson (pedigree child)

Ancestor 12.0 with third wife:

> 12.0   Henry Johnson
> 12.0*3   Henrietta Wilson
>   6.5   Frank Johnson
>   6.6   Fred Johnson

In the above examples it is important to separate these families, creating separate family group sheets — then the birth order and ID numbers for each member of the family can be assigned, and it will be easier to follow.

The same technique can be used if ancestor 13.0 had a previous marriage with children. Here is an example:

> 13.0*1   Joshua Williams
> 13.0   Martha (–––––)
>   6.7   Henry Williams
>   6.8   Elizabeth Williams

If Martha (–––––) were the mother of children by a previous marriage, the children should have a number indicating a close relationship with ancestor 6.0 — because these children would be half-brothers or half-sisters of an ancestor. Therefore, the combined pool of collateral children for either the father or mother should be used in assigning these ID numbers. Martha (———-) 13.0 did not have eight children — but both she and Henry Jones (12.0) combined had eight children. All of these children should have an ID number based on, and related to, ancestor 6.0, a brother or half-brother to all the other children of either parent.

What About Step-Children?

There is also a way of assigning ID numbers to spouses and children from a previous marriage of Joshua Williams, above:

> 13.0*1   Joshua Williams
> 13.0* 1/*1 Helen White
>   13.0*1/1 James Williams
>   13.0*1/2 Mary Williams

In Helen White's ID number above, the slash (/) acts as a separator and indicates a previous or later spouse. Since Joshua Williams received his number as the first spouse of 13.0 (an ancestor), he is given an ID 13.0*1, so any number for an earlier or later spouse needs another asterisk. The children of this union have ID numbers assigned in similar fashion as other collaterals — but using a slash (/) and a number indicating birth order for each.

What About Adopted Children?

If you wish to include an adopted child in a sibling list, assign an ID number as if the adopted child were one of the siblings — but it is very important to note that a person was adopted. If the adopted child's birth parents are known, then another family group sheet may be needed to show the relationships. In such cases, the adopted child may appear on two family group sheets, and a cross-referencing note on each family sheet should clarify the facts regarding the adoption.

Descendants of Number One

Assigning ahnentafel numbers works well for the ancestors and collaterals of number one. But what if you decide to make yourself number one in the pedigree? How do you give a number to your spouse? Your children? Your grandchildren? Here are suggestions for assigning ID numbers to a spouse and children of number one:

Family of Samuel Johnson, the genealogist:

> 1.0   Samuel Johnson, Sr.
> 1.0*   Mary Smith
>> 1.01   Samuel Johnson, Jr.
>> 1.02   John Johnson
>> 1.03   Mary Johnson
>> 1.04   William Johnson

Family of William Johnson, a son of Samuel Johnson, Sr.:

> 1.04   William Johnson
> 1.04*   Millie Gray
>> 1.041   Elizabeth Johnson
>> 1.042   Wilma Johnson
>> 1.043   Frank Johnson

A genealogist doing the work may find this next example works just as well. If you wish to make your child number 1.0 — or if you have more than one child, assign IDs as 1.1, 1.2, 1.3, and so on — then you and your spouse would be 2.0 and 3.0. The pedigree would be identical for each of your children as a different person in the number one position.

For example:

> 2.0   John Doe
> 3.0   Mary Roe
>> 1.1   William Doe
>> 1.2   Martha Doe
>> 1.3   Martin Doe

Note that none of the children are 1.0, but any could be in the number one position on a pedigree chart. Now, any of the children could be shown as a parent on a family group sheet as in the example below:

> 1.2*1   Frank Smith
> 1.2   Martha Doe
>> 1.21   Helen Smith (twin)
>> 1.22   Ellen Smith (twin)
>> 1.23   Farley Smith

ID Numbers in a Computer Database

Finally, if you have followed along so far, there has to be a good reason for this numbering madness — the idea of assigning ID numbers for anyone. Entering the ahnentafel/collateral numbers into a computer is one way to demonstrate the effectiveness of having ID numbers for any person important to the genealogical project.

With a computer, a genealogist can prepare a list of every person collected, whether they are ancestors, siblings of ancestors, or collateral descendants. Computers have a pre-defined order in which alpha characters, numbers, and symbols are sorted, following something called the ASCII code (which is just a table of characters with a numerical value assigned to each character).

Here is a table of ID numbers, names, and relationships from my own pedigree and collateral relatives. This list shows the way the names could be sorted in a computer, based on the ID numbers. But, the same list can also be sorted in alphabetical order by the surnames. In either sort, the list provides a complete list of ancestors, siblings of ancestors, as well as collateral descendants. Without the ID numbers, you would have a list of names. With the ID numbers, you have an indication of the relationship of any person to the person who is number one in a pedigree.

Ancestors and Collaterals of William Dollarhide

ID No.	Name	Relationship to No. 1
1.0	William Dollarhide	me
1.0*1	Mary (Smith) Pipitone	my first wife
1.0*/*1	Gerald Pipitone	my first wife's first husband
1.0*/1	Loren Pipitone	my step-daughter
1.0*/2	Jerry Pipitone	my step-son
1.0*1:2	Winston Smith	my first wife's father
1.0*1:3	Olive Stovall	my first wife's mother
1.01	Meredith Dollarhide	my daughter
1.01*	Robert Cotton	my son-in-law
1.01*:2	Dewayne Cotton	my son-in-law's father
1.01*:3	Norma Davis	my son-in-law's mother
1.011	Jace Austin Cotton	my grandson
1.0*2.0	Linda Lawson	my second wife
1.0*2.1	Michael Lawson	my second wife's brother
1.0*2.2	Leroy T. Lawson	my second wife's father
1.0*2.3	Flora C. Cisna	my second wife's mother
1.1	Eunice L. Dollarhide	my sister
1.1*1	Kenneth Stumpf	my sister's first husband
1.1*2	Louis Stearns	my sister's second husband
1.11	Margie Stumpf	my niece, my sister's daughter
1.11*1	Frederick Litt	my niece's first husband
1.11*2	Steven Mowles	my niece's second husband
1.111	Aaron Litt	my nephew, my sister's son

1.112	Melissa Mowles	my grand-niece
1.12	Kim B. Stumpf	my nephew, my sister's son
1.2	Norman L. Dollarhide	my brother
1.2*1	Pearl Birchett	my brother's first wife
1.2*2	Meredith Schauss	my brother's second wife
1.21	Kevin L. Dollarhide	my nephew
1.22	Leslie Dollarhide	my nephew
1.23	Michael Dollarhide	my nephew
1.24	Robert Dollarhide	my nephew
1.3	Richard Dollarhide	my brother
1.4	David Dollarhide	my brother
1.4*	Virginia Olson	my sister-in-law
1.41	Crystal Dollarhide	my niece, my brother's daughter
1.42	Wenda Dollarhide	my niece, my brother's daughter
1.42*1	Ricky Zonnefeld	my niece's husband
1.421	Jesse Zonnefeld	my grand-nephew
1.5	James C. Dollarhide	my brother
1.5*	Kathleen Hansen	my sister-in-law
1.51	Robin Dollarhide	my niece, my brother's daughter
1.51*1	Gregory Takemoto	my niece's husband
1.512	Kearstyn Takemoto	my grand-niece
1.6	Leonard L. Dollarhide	my brother
1.6*1	Georgia Dengle	my brother's first wife
1.6*2	Susan Cox	my brother's second wife
2.0	Albert R. Dollarhide	my father
2.1	Leonard L. Dollarhide	my uncle, my father's brother
3.0	Marjory W. Wiles	my mother
3.2	Frances Wiles	my aunt, my mother's sister
4.0	John C. Dollarhide	my paternal grandfather

. . . and so on . . .

Note that collateral persons can be inserted in numerical order at any point. The ID numbers allow a genealogist to sort and organize the names in an integrated scheme. The combined pedigree and collateral positions are unlimited.

Genealogists have the means of using ID numbers for ancestors, collaterals, and their descendants. For a pedigree, ahnentafel numbers identify each direct ancestor with a unique ID number which can then be used for organizing and filing genealogical documentation related to that person. ID numbers connected to these ahnentafel numbers allow for sorting, finding, and retrieving information quickly.

Descendancy Numbering Systems

The Register System

The Register System is a descendancy numbering system first used by the New England Historic Genealogical Society in their periodical, *The New England Historical and Genealogical Register* — hence, the name. As an example of the Register System, the following partial descendancy was taken from a book published in 1984 by the Genealogical Publishing Company — *American Ancestors and Cousins of the Princess of Wales*, by Gary Boyd Roberts and William Addams Reitwiesner (extracted from page 92):

Descendants of Franklin H. Work and of Ellen Wood
(great-great-grandparents of The Princess of Wales)

1. FRANKLIN H. WORK, dry goods merchant, stockbroker, b. Chillicothe, Ohio, 10 Feb. 1819, d. New York, N.Y., 16 March 1911, son of John Wark and of Sarah Duncan Boude, m. New York, N.Y., 19 Feb. 1857, Ellen Wood, b. Chillicothe, Ohio, 18 July 1831, d. New York, N.Y., 22 Feb. 1877, dau. of John Wood and of Eleanor Strong.

Issue: (surname WORK):

2. a. Frances Eleanor, b. New York, N.Y., 27 Oct 1857, d. New York, N.Y., 26 Jan 1947.
   b. George Paul, b. 8 Sept. 1858, d. Davos Platz, Kt. Grisons (Switz.), 25 Feb. 1900.
3. c. Lucy Bond, b. New York, N.Y., May 1860, d. New York, N.Y., 21 March 1934.

2. FRANCES ELEANOR WORK, b. New York, N.Y., 27 Oct 1857, d. New York, N.Y., 26 Jan. 1947, m. (1) New York, N.Y., 22 Sept. 1880, div. Wilmington, Del., 3 March 1891, James Boothby BURKE ROCHE, from 10 Sept.,1856, Hon. James Boothby BURKE ROCHE, from 1 Sept. 1920, 3rd Baron Fermoy, b. Twyford Abbey, Middx., 28 July 1851, d. Westminster, 30 Oct. 1920, son of Edmund BURKE ROCHE, 1st Baron Fermoy, and of Eliza Caroline BOOTHBY; m. (2) New York, N.Y., 4 Aug. 1905, div. New York, 5 Nov. 1909, as his second wife, Aurel BATONYI [he had m. (1) and div.], son of Leopold BATONYI.

2. FRANCES ELEANOR WORK, Continued:

Issue by first husband (surname BURKE ROCHE); styled from 1 Sept. 1920 "Hon.":

   a. Eileen, b. 1882, d. 1882
4. b. Cynthia, b. London, 10 Apr. 1884, d. Newport, R.I., 18 Dec 1966.
5. c. Edmund Maurice, b. Chelsea, 15 May 1885, [twin], d. King's Lynn, 8 July 1955.
   d. Francis George, b. Chelsea, 15 May 1885, [twin], d. Newport, R.I., 30 Oct 1958.

3. LUCY BOND WORK, b. New York, N.Y. May 1860, d. New York, N.Y., 21 March 1934, m. New York, N.Y., 27 Apr. 1887.
   ...more...

In the above example, the Register numbers were assigned with the first person as number 1, followed by his children as 2, 3, 4, etc. Not every person is assigned a number, however, just those who will be continued with their line of descent shown later. Of the three children of Franklin Work listed above as Frances, George, and Lucy, just two have been assigned numbers. Because George has no number assigned, we presume the authors chose not to continue the descent-line of George Paul Work (which is the prerogative of the author).

There are two columns of information shown. The left margin indicates the adult descent line, while the indented column indicates the children in their order of birth, thus:

1. Franklin Work
   2. a. Frances Eleanor Work
      b. George Paul Work
3. c. Lucy Bond Work

2. Frances Eleanor Work

Except for the first progenitor, every person given a number will appear first as a child, the number indicating his/her position in the adult descent line. If no number is given, that will be the last time that child will be mentioned in the descendancy.

In the child column, brief vitals are listed. But in the adult column, more detail about the person is given, generally including the birthplace and date, then the death date and place, followed by any marriages. This is also the place where any biographical information about the person would appear — although the above example has little biographical text. There is no limit to the length of vitals and biographical data that can be included in the adult column listing for a person — this is the standard method of producing a family history in book form.

The birth order for the children, in this case, was indicated with lower case a, b, c, etc. But the birth order can also be indicated with lower case roman numerals, such as i, ii, iii, for example:

1. Franklin Work
2. i. Frances Eleanor Work
   ii. George Paul Work
3. iii. Lucy Bond Work

Note that the children without a Register number will not appear again. Because the numbers continue to rise, and because there are only two columns of numbers to follow, the Register System can be very easy to read, even if the numbers are quite large due to a great number of descendants. For example, say a book were opened in the middle and the numbers appeared as shown below:

3245. James Brown

    6641. i. William Brown
    6642. ii. Elizabeth Brown
    6643. iii. Mary Brown

3246. Wilma Brown

This may seem confusing at first; but by understanding the Register System, several rules apply. To find the parents of James Brown, No. 3245, move to the child column and start turning pages toward the front of the book until a child appears with that number. Immediately above that list of children, the parents will be listed. On the other hand, to find William Brown, No. 6641, as an adult, move to the adult column and start turning pages towards the back of the book. The numbers in both columns are sequential, and all children listed (with a number) will appear in both columns.

Although this system is widely used and accepted by genealogists in the U.S., there are some fatal flaws built into the Register System. First, the spouse of a descendant receives no number at all — only the blood-line descendants are assigned numbers in the Register System. Moreover, the assignment of register numbers is dangerous, particularly when further research may reveal the existence of more children of a person. Adding people to the list means that the entire list must be renumbered from that point, or children within a family grouping must be numbered out of sequence.

The Register System is the accepted standard for a number of periodicals in America besides the *New England Historical and Genealogical Register*.

Many of these periodicals accept manuscripts from genealogists for publication, but one must conform to the Register System or the editors will not even read the manuscript. Therefore, if a goal is to prepare an article for a national magazine, an understanding of the Register System is important.

The Modified Register System

A variation of the Register System was adapted first by the *New York Biographical and Genealogical Record* and became known as the Record System. The same variation was also adopted by the *National Genealogical Society Quarterly*. The New York periodical has since returned to the older New England Register method, while the National Genealogical Society's periodical now refers to its descendancy numbering scheme as the Modified Register System.

Here is an outline of the same Work family descendancy using the Modified Register System:

1. Franklin Work

  + 2. i. Frances Eleanor Work
      3. ii. George Paul Work
  + 4. iii. Lucy Bond Work

2. Frances Eleanor Work
   (m. Burke Roche)

      5. i. Eileen Burke Roche
+ 6. ii. Cynthia Burke Roche
+ 7. iii. Edmund Maurice Burke Roche
      8. iv. Francis George Burke Roche

Unlike the Register System, in the Modified Register System, every person receives a Register number, an arabic number indicating the line of descent. Every person also receives a lower case roman numeral indicating their birth order within a family grouping. But, unique to the Modified Register System is a symbol that indicates if a child is to be repeated as an adult. The + (plus sign) is normally used for this purpose. Even though every child may have a Register number, if no + (plus sign) appears, that will be the last time that particular name will be seen in the descendancy. To some genealogists, the Modified Register System is considered superior to the Register System because every descendant receives a number.

However, in both systems, only the blood-line descendants of number 1 receive a Register number. Spouses of descendants are not part of the descendancy and receive no number at all. A genealogist can review these numbering systems in greater detail by visiting a genealogical library with a family history section. Many published books have a numbering system similar or identical to the Register or Modified Register system described above. Variations of these numbering systems exist as well, but again, if the goal is to publish a genealogical article for a national magazine, these two numbering systems should be followed as closely as possible.

Common Features and Differences Between The Two Systems

A standard method for showing the generation for each adult in both the Register and Modified Register systems is to use superscripts after their first names, for example:

1. Franklin[1] Work

    + 2. i. Frances Eleanor[2] Work
       3. ii. George Paul Work
    + 4. iii. Lucy Bond Work

2. Frances Eleanor[2] Work (Franklin[1])
   (m. Burke Roche)

      5. i. Eileen[3] Burke Roche
+ 6. ii. Cynthia Burke Roche
+ 7. iii. Edmund Maurice Burke Roche
      8. iv. Francis George Burke Roche

For each person identified in the adult column, the superscript indicates the generation of that person removed from number 1. Following the person's name, the first names and superscripts for each step in the line of descent back to number 1 can be given in parentheses. The generation superscript for the first child in a list of children need not be repeated for the remaining children.

An example of an adult in the fifth generation of a descendancy might be as shown below. Note that in the New England Historic Genealogical Society's *Register*, adult names are shown in all capitals, while in the Modified Register system, the adult names are in upper/lower case, as well as shown in bold lettering (the method preferred by the National Genealogical Society's *Quarterly*).

NEHGS Register System:

312. WILLIAM HENRY^5 SMITH, JR. (William Henry, Sr.^{4}, James^3, Henry^2, Willard^1)

NGS Modified Register System:

355. **William Henry^5 Smith, Jr.** (William Henry, Sr.^{4}, James^3, Henry^2, Willard^1)

Generally, the Register System uses a superscript ^{1} to indicate the first American progenitor and then employs superscript letters after names to indicate foreign ancestors preceding the American genealogy. For example, if James Smith, Jr. were the first American immigrant and progenitor, his name and British lineage in parentheses could be shown as follows:

1. JAMES^1 SMITH, JR. (James, Sr.^{A}, William^B)

Another difference in style between the two systems is in the narrative writing. The NEHGS Register System allows abbreviations in text — the NGS Modified Register encourages readable text with no abbreviations.

Writing style used in the NEHGS Register System:

1. FRANKLIN H. WORK, dry goods merchant, stockbroker, b. Chillicothe, Ohio, 10 Feb. 1819, d. New York, N.Y., 16 March 1911, son of John Wark and of Sarah Duncan Boude, m. New York, N.Y., 19 Feb. 1857, Ellen Wood, b. Chillicothe, Ohio, 18 July 1831, d. New York, N.Y., 22 Feb. 1877, dau. of John Wood and of Eleanor Strong.

Writing style used in NGS Modified Register System:

1. **Franklin H. Work,** son of John Wark and of Sarah Duncan Boude, born 10 February 1819 in Chillicothe, Ohio; died 16 March 1911 in New York City. He was married 19 February 1857 in New Nork City to **Ellen Wood**, daughter of John Wood and of Eleanor Strong, born 18 July 1831 in Chillicothe, Ohio; died 22 February 1877 in New York City. Franklin Work was a dry goods merchant and stockbroker...

The Henry System

Reginald Buchanan Henry, M.D., born in 1881, was a physician and genealogist. In his book, *Genealogies of the Families of the Presidents* (Rutland, VT: The Tuttle Co., 1935), Dr. Henry presented a numbering scheme to show the descendants of the Presidential families featured in his book. Although there were earlier genealogists who came up with a similar numbering scheme for a descendancy, Dr. Henry's book was a well known genealogy book published which employed this particular method of numbering descendants. For that reason, genealogists today using this numbering scheme refer to it as "The Henry System."

The Henry System differs radically from the Register or Modified Register numbering systems. While the Register system employs an arabic number assigned to each descendant, the numbers are consecutive and supply only an identification of a person in a descendancy. The numbers in the Henry System, on the other hand, are more meaningful because, by looking at a person's number only, a relative position in the descendancy can be determined, i.e., the number of generations removed from the first progenitor, the birth order of the person, and the lineage of the person back to the first progenitor.

Using the same family from our previous article, here is an example of the Henry System:

1 Franklin Work

	11	Frances Eleanor Work
	12	George Paul Work
	13	Lucy Bond Work

11 Frances Eleanor Work
(m. Burke Roche)

111 Eileen Burke Roche
112 Cynthia Burke Roche
113 Edmund Maurice Burke Roche
114 Francis George Burke Roche

In this system, the number identifies the blood-line descendant, as well as the lineage back to number 1. Each number is a discrete identification number, an indication of the birth order, and the number of generations removed from the person who starts the descendancy.

Franklin Work, as number 1, starts the descendancy. His first child was Frances Eleanor Work. Her number repeats Franklin's number and then gives her birth order, express as a 1. Thus, her number is 11 (spoken as "one-one," not "eleven"). The 4th child of Frances Eleanor Work was Francis George whose number repeats his mother's number (11), then adds a number indicating his birth order (114)… and so on.

The previous example has repeated the two-column arrangement, but this is not a required feature of the Henry System. For example, a descendancy could be tabulated in chart form as in the example shown below:

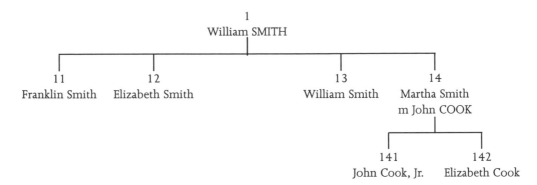

To extend the descendancy using descendant number 142, Elizabeth Cook, her children would be 1421, 1422, 1423, and so on. The descent comes down on either males or females but is based on the blood-line descendants only. Therefore, as was true in the Register or Modified Register systems, the spouses who marry into the descendancy do not receive a number assignment in the Henry System.

With the Henry System, an ID number is possible for a person such as 1559856. To understand this number, read from right to left: the 6th child, of the 5th child, of the 8th child, of the 9th child, of the 5th child, of the 5th child, of number 1. The descent from number 1 to the person 1559856 is as follows:

1
  15
    155
      1559
        15598
          155985
          1559856

Therefore, to trace the lineage back to the progenitor, just remove the last digit to find the number of the person's blood-line parent. One digit is one generation.

However, there is a problem with the Henry numbers if there are more than 9 children in a family. This is because each digit is meant to represent one generation. To have a "13" for a thirteenth child, the double digits would cause the numbers to go awry. So, there are some methods a genealogist can use to indicate a person who was in a family with more than 9 children.

In the example above, say that the 9th child should have been the 13th child:

    Method 1:   1-5-5-13-8-5-6 (all generations separated)
    Method 2:   155(13)856 (double digits only separated)
    Method 3:   155-13-856 (" " " ")
    Method 4:   155D856 (Alpha characters for 10 or higher)

Any of the above will solve the problem of double digits but the one that is probably the most useful is Method 4, particularly if a genealogist plans on entering such numbers into a computer. The "D" in Method 4 represents the 13th child.

Hexadecimal numbers have a base of 16 rather than 10 as in decimal numbers and use alpha characters to extend the number to the 16th position. But, using alpha characters for the 10th or higher numbers in the Henry System is not really a hexadecimal system, it is just a technique to assign single digit numbers. (The numerical positions in a hexadecimal system are not the same.)

A comparison of decimal numbers with extended Henry numbers is as follows:

Number of children in a family

Decimal	Henry
1	1
2	2
3	3
4	4
5	5
6	6
7	7
8	8
9	9
10	A
11	B
12	C
13	D
14	E
15	F
16	G
17	H
...and so on...	

Using alpha characters for the 10th and later children in a family solves the problem of double digit numbers as part of the Henry numbering system because every numerical position/generation is back to one digit again.

Part III
Blank Forms

Genealogical Forms for Copying:

Family Data Sheet   Surname: FDS No.

Date: Researcher:

| ❑ Book | ❑ Periodical | ❑ Microfilm | ❑ Other | Author/Editor: |

Title/Article:

| In/By: | | Vol. | No. | Page | Publisher: |

| DATA OBTAINED FROM: | ❑ Library | ❑ Correspondence* | ❑ Field Research | ❑ Oral Dictation | ❑ Family Record |

| CENSUS: | ❑ Soundex | ❑ Schedules | Series | Roll | ED | Sheet | Fam. No. |

| Year | State | County | Township | Subdistrict |

* Received From: ❑ Indexed

Family Data Sheet   Surname: *DOLLARHIDE*   FDS No. *CA-13*

Date: *4 Jan 1999*   Researcher: *Wm. Dollarhide*

☐ Book   ☐ Periodical   ☒ Microfilm   ☐ Other   Author/Editor:

Title/Article: *1900 Fed. Census - California*

In/By: *Nat'l Archives - Seattle*   Vol.   No.   Page   Publisher:

DATA OBTAINED FROM: ☒ Library   ☐ Correspondence*   ☐ Field Research   ☐ Oral Dictation   ☐ Family Record

CENSUS: ☐ Soundex   ☒ Schedules   Series *7623*   Roll *113*   ED *133*   Sheet *4*   Fam. No. *7B*

Year *1900*   State *CA*   County *Siskiyou*   Township *Ft. Jones*   Subdistrict *Scott Valley*

in town of Ft. Jones, calif.:
living in a rented house:

DOLLARHIDE, John, age 42, b. Mar 1858 in Iowa
(head)   parents b. Indiana
*   occupation: teamster*
*   married 13 years*

wife: Addie, age 31, b. Mar 1869 in Oregon
*   parents b. Missouri*
*   married 13 years*
*   mother of 6 ch, 4 living*

Children:

*   1. Charles L., age 12, b. Jan 1888 in Calif.*

*   2. Harry L., age 10, b. Aug 1890 in Calif.*

*   3. John C., age 5, b. Sep 1895 in Calif.*

*   4. Dewie A. (female), age 2, b. Apr 1898 in Calif.*

Also in Household:

DOLLARHIDE, Samuel (Brother) b. Aug 1852 in Iowa
*   parents b. Indiana*
*   occupation: Teamster*
*   single*

* Received From: ☒ Indexed

Family Data Sheet. The use of this form as discussed in Essay 4, "Organizing the Paper." This form can be used to gather genealogical references from any source. As a means of collecting sources on the same size sheet, the form will help organize your reference materials. It is suggested that all genealogical research notes be gathered on the same sheet size so they can be organized in notebooks or file folders.

Family Group Sheet

Father FULL NAME:

EVENT	DAY MONTH YEAR	PLACE OF EVENT	(City, Township, County, State, or Country)
Birth			
Marriage			
Death			
Burial			

NOTES:

His Other Spouse (s):

| His Father: | | Born | | Died | |
| His Mother: | | Born | | Died | |

Mother FULL MAIDEN NAME:

EVENT	DAY MONTH YEAR	PLACE OF EVENT	(City, Township, County, Staty, or Country)
Birth			
Death			
Burial			

NOTES:

Her Other Spouse (s):

| Her Father: | | Born | | Died | |
| Her Mother: | | Born | | Died | |

Children (given names)

		DAY MONTH YEAR	PLACE OF EVENT	NAME OF SPOUSE (s)
1	b			
	m			
	d			
2	b			
	m			
	d			
3	b			
	m			
	d			
4	b			
	m			
	d			
5	b			
	m			
	d			
6	b			
	m			
	d			
7	b			
	m			
	d			
8	b			
	m			
	d			
9	b			
	m			
	d			
10	b			
	m			
	d			
11	b			
	m			
	d			
12	b			
	m			
	d			

REFERENCES:

Family Group Sheet

Father FULL NAME: John Conrad DOLLARHIDE

EVENT	DAY MONTH YEAR	PLACE OF EVENT (City, Township, County, State, or Country)
Birth	17 Mar 1858	Des Moines, Polk Co., Iowa
Marriage	18 Sep 1887	Pittville, Shasta Co., Calif.
Death	7 Jun 1934	Pt. Angeles, Clallam Co., WA
Burial	10 Jun 1934	Oceanview Cemetery, Pt. Angeles, WA

NOTES: Came to Calif. via Wagon Train, age 2. Worked as a teamster most of his life

His Other Spouse (s): None

His Father: Rev. John DOLLARHIDE Born 1814 IN Died 1869 CA

His Mother: Lucy Ann REYNOLDS Born 1820 OH Died 1892 CA

Mother FULL MAIDEN NAME: Addie McNAMER

EVENT	DAY MONTH YEAR	PLACE OF EVENT (City, Township, County, State, or Country)
Birth	20 Mar 1869	Salem, Marion Co., OR
Death	19 Feb 1944	Seattle, King Co., WA
Burial	24 Feb 1944	Oceanview Cemetery, Pt. Angeles, WA

NOTES:

Her Other Spouse (s): None

Her Father: John Hurley McNEMAR Born 1848 IA Died 1922 OR

Her Mother: Amanda Jane MAYFIELD Born 1852 IA Died 1931 WA

Children (given names)		DAY MONTH YEAR	PLACE OF EVENT	NAME OF SPOUSE (s)
1 Charles Leonard	b	21 Jan 1888	Susanville, Lassen Co., CA	Belle BUNDY
	m	1908	Dayton, Columbia Co., WA	
	d	6 Nov 1965	Pt. Angeles, Callam Co., WA	
2 Ann	b	Sep 1889	Pittville, Shasta Co., CA	died young, never married
	m			
	d	Oct 1889	Pittville, Shasta Co., CA	
3 Harry Leroy	b	24 Aug 1890	Pittville, Shasta Co., CA	never married
	m			
	d	Mar 1945	Pt. Angeles, Clallam Co., WA	
4 Matthew (Mattie)	b	6 Nov 1893	Stockton, San Joaquin Co., CA	died young, never married
	m			
	d	Mar 1894	Shasta Co., CA (?)	
5 John Clifford	b	11 Sep 1895	Mt. Shasta, Siskiyou Co., CA	1. Margaret McNAMER 2. Nina FOSTER 3. Cecil FISHER 4. Thelma Rhode Ellis
	m (1)	7 Jul 1917	Walla Walla, WA	
	d	17 Aug 1950	Everett, Snohomish Co., WA	
6 Dewie Austine	b	20 Aug 1898	Ft. Jones, Siskiyou Co., CA	John Edwin FERNLEAF (Jack)
	m	1920	Dayton, Columbia Co., WA	
	d	Jun 1981	Eureka, Humboldt Co., CA	
7 Lesley Herman	b	28 Sep 1900	Medford, Jackson Co., OR	1. Neva ZINN 2. Margaret ____
	m (1)	23 Jun 1920	Walla Walla, WA	
	d	17 Apr 1967	Portland, Multnomah Co., OR	
8 Mable Clare	b	18 Jan 1903	Crescent City, Del Norte Co., CA	1. George PARK 2. David JONES 3. Cal HARTMAN
	m (1)	1929	Pt. Angeles, Clallam Co., WA	
	d			
9 Albert Raymond	b	19 Apr 1905	Oakland, Douglas Co., OR	Marjory Watkins WILES
	m	18 Jan 1930	Puyallup, Pierce Co., WA	
	d	18 Mar 1977	Blaine, Whatcom Co., WA	
10 Zelma Wilmia	b	18 Sep 1907	Dayton, Columbia Co., WA	died age 14. never married
	m			
	d	30 Dec 1921	Dayton, Columbia Co., WA	
11 Ethel Leota (Tootsie)	b	6 Sep 1911	Dayton, Columbia Co., WA	Albert Francis PADGETTE
	m	1924	Pt. Angeles, Clallam Co., WA	
	d			
12	b			
	m			
	d			

REFERENCES:

Family Group Sheet. (12 children). This one-sided form allows for identifying the important facts about the members of one family, with space for up to 12 children. Dates should be written in the military style, e.g., 12 Feb 1955. Places of births, marriages, and deaths should be as complete as possible, including a town, city, county, and state (or country, if other than the U.S.).

Family Group Sheet

Father FULL NAME:

EVENT	DAY MONTH YEAR	PLACE OF EVENT	(City, Township, County, State, or Country)
Birth			
Marriage			
Death			
Burial			

NOTES:

His Other Spouse (s):

His Father:	Born	Died
His Mother:	Born	Died

Mother FULL MAIDEN NAME:

EVENT	DAY MONTH YEAR	PLACE OF EVENT	(City, Township, County, Staty, or Country)
Birth			
Death			
Burial			

NOTES:

Her Other Spouse (s):

Her Father:	Born	Died
Her Mother:	Born	Died

Children (given names)

		DAY MONTH YEAR	PLACE OF EVENT	NAME OF SPOUSE (s)
1	b			
	m			
	d			
2	b			
	m			
	d			
3	b			
	m			
	d			
4	b			
	m			
	d			
5	b			
	m			
	d			
6	b			
	m			
	d			
7	b			
	m			
	d			
8	b			
	m			
	d			

Family Group Sheet

Father FULL NAME: _John Conrad DOLLARHIDE_

EVENT	DAY MONTH YEAR	PLACE OF EVENT (City, Township, County, State, or Country)
Birth	17 Mar 1858	Des Moines, Polk Co., IA
Marriage	18 Sep 1887	Pittville, Shasta Co., CA
Death	7 Jun 1934	Port Angeles, Clallam Co., WA
Burial	10 Jun 1934	Oceanview Cemetery, Pt. Angeles, WA

NOTES: _Came to Calif. via Wagon Train at age 2. Worked as a teamster most of life._

His Other Spouse (s): _None_

His Father: _Rev. John DOLLARHIDE_   Born _1814 IN_   Died _1869 CA_

His Mother: _Lucy Ann REYNOLDS_   Born _1820 OH_   Died _1892 CA_

Mother FULL MAIDEN NAME: _Addie McNAMER_

EVENT	DAY MONTH YEAR	PLACE OF EVENT (City, Township, County, State, or Country)
Birth	20 March 1869	Salem, Marion Co., OR
Death	19 Feb 1944	Seattle, King Co., WA
Burial	24 Feb 1944	Oceanview Cemetery, Pt. Angeles, WA

NOTES: _Changed spelling of name McNEMAR to McNAMER in 1870's_

Her Other Spouse (s): _None_

Her Father: _John Hurley McNEMAR_   Born _1848 IA_   Died _1922 OR_

Her Mother: _Amanda Jane MAYFIELD_   Born _1852 IA_   Died _1931 WA_

Children (given names)		DAY MONTH YEAR	PLACE OF EVENT	NAME OF SPOUSE (s)
1 Charles Leonard	b	21 Jan 1888	Susanville, Lassen Co. CA	Belle BUNDY
	m	1908	Dayton, Columbia Co., WA	
	d	6 Nov 1965	Pt. Angeles, Clallam Co., WA	
2 Ann	b	Sep 1889	Pittville, Shasta Co., CA	died as infant
	m	—	" " "	
	d	Oct 1889	" " "	
3 Harry Leroy (Roy)	b	24 Aug 1890	Pittville (?) Shasta Co. CA	Never married
	m	—		
	d	Mar 1945	Pt. Angeles, Clallam Co., WA	
4 Matthew (Mattie)	b	6 Nov 1893	Stockton, San Joaquin Co CA	died as infant
	m	—		
	d	Mar 1894	Shasta Co. (?) CA	
5 John Clifford (Cliff)	b	11 Sep 1895	Mt. Shasta, Siskiyou Co. CA	2) Nina FOSTER
	m	4 marriages 1) Margaret McNAMER		3) Cecil FISHER
	d	17 Aug 1950	Everett, Snohomish Co., WA	4) Thelma Rhode Ellis
6 Dewie Austine (female)	b	20 Aug 1898	Ft. Jones, Siskiyou Co., CA	John Edwin (Jack)
	m	ca 1920	Dayton, Columbia Co., WA	FERNLEAF
	d	Jun 1981	Eureka, Humboldt Co., CA	
7 Lesley Herman	b	28 Sep 1900	Medford, Jackson Co., OR	1) Neva ZINN
	m	1) 23 Jun 1920	Walla Walla, WA	2) Margaret (——)
	d	17 Apr 1967	Portland, Multnomah Co., OR	
8 Mable Clare (Mamie)	b	18 Jan 1903	Crescent	1) George PARK
	m	1) 1929	Pt. Angeles, WA	2) David JONES
	d			3) Cal Hartman

Continued, 3 more children

Family Group Sheet. (8 children). This form allows for identifying the important facts about the members of one family, with space for up to 8 children. Adding a continuation sheet, either on the back side of this sheet or as added one-side sheets will allow for more than 9 children and more references.

Continuation, Family of

Children (continued)		DAY MONTH YEAR	PLACE OF EVENT	NAME OF SPOUSE (s)
9	b			
	m			
	d			
10	b			
	m			
	d			
11	b			
	m			
	d			
12	b			
	m			
	d			

References   Itemize each source used to document names, dates, and places for each member of the family

Page/Source	Type of Record	In Reference To	Information Given

Continuation, Family of *John and Addie (McNAMEE) DOLLARHIDE*

Children (continued)		DAY MONTH YEAR	PLACE OF EVENT	NAME OF SPOUSE (s)
9 Albert Raymond	b	19 Apr 1906	Oakland, Douglas Co., OR	Marjory Watkins WILES
	m	18 Jan 1930	Puyallup, Pierce Co., WA	
	d	18 Mar 1977	Blaine, Whatcom Co., WA	
10 Zelma Wilmia	b	18 Sep 1907	Dayton, Columbia Co., WA	
	m	Never married		
	d	30 Dec 1921	Dayton, Columbia Co., WA	
11 Ethel Leota (Tootsie)	b	6 Sep 1911	Dayton, Columbia Co., WA	Albert Francis PADGETTE
	m	ca 1929	Pt. Angeles, Clallam Co., WA	
	d			
12	b			
	m			
	d			

References   Itemize each source used to document names, dates, and places for each member of the family

Page/Source	Type of Record	In Reference To	Information Given
CA 13	1900 Census	John Conrad	birth, res
CA 21	Marriage Cert.	" "	date/place of marriage, Addie's Father
WA 10	Obituary	" "	birth, death, survivors
WA 13	Death Cert.	" "	birth, death, parents
CA 40	1870 Census	" "	child of re., w/mother, Lucy
WA 8	Rural Directory	" "	Res in Columbia Co., WA 1910-11
WA 6	City Directory	John Conrad,	res. in Pt. Angeles, WA 1923
"	"	Charles L.,	" "
"	"	Harry Leroy,	" "
"	"	Lesley, and	" "
"	"	Albert R.	" "
CA 112	Land Patent	John C.	1901 Shasta Co CA
CA 113	" "	" "	1903 Siskiyou Co CA
WA 43	Birth Cert.	Albert R.	"Baby Boy" parents not named
CA 152	Delayed Birth Cert.	" "	filed in 1945 w/affidavits of sisters.
WA 81	Funeral Program	John Clifford	birth, death
WA 26	Military Papers	Harry Leroy	Discharge, dates of service, WWI
WA 9	Photograph	Family	John, Addie, 9 children ca 1921 in Dayton, WA
OR-32	Obituary	Lesley H.	birth, death, marriage, children
WA 12	Marriage Record	John Clifford	m. to his cousin, Margaret McNamee, 1919
WA 16	Marriage Record	Albert R.	to Marjory WILES 1930
WA 17	Driver's License	" "	birth, res. in Eureka, CA 1945
WA 101	Funeral Program	" "	birth, death, parents
WA 102	Obituary	" "	" " " , survivors

Family Group Sheet Continuation Sheet. (9 thru 12 children). This form is designed to be used with the Family Group Sheet which has up to 8 children. This sheet can be printed to the backside of the first form, or used as another one-sided sheet.

Continuation, Family of _____

Children (continued)		DAY MONTH YEAR	PLACE OF EVENT	NAME OF SPOUSE (s)
9	b			
	m			
	d			
10	b			
	m			
	d			
11	b			
	m			
	d			
12	b			
	m			
	d			
13	b			
	m			
	d			
14	b			
	m			
	d			
15	b			
	m			
	d			

References Itemize each source used to document names, dates, and places for each member of the family

Page/Source	Type of Record	In Reference To	Information Given

Continuation, Family of _Rev. John and Lucy (REYNOLDS) DOLLARHIDE_

Children (continued)		DAY MONTH YEAR	PLACE OF EVENT	NAME OF SPOUSE (s)
9 Merinda	b	9 Apr 1851	Jasper Co., IN	—
	m	—		
	d	25 Aug 1851	Jasper Co., IN	
10 Samuel Walker	b	28 Aug 1852	Illinois	—
	m	—	never married	
	d	18 Sep 1909	Fall River Mills, Shasta Co., CA	
11 Loretta Lucy	b	21 Feb 1854	Illinois	David S. KEENER
	m	5 May 1870	Butte Co., CA	
	d	27 Mar 1929	Oroville, Butte Co., CA	
12 Lawrence	b	9 Apr 1856	Fayette Co., IA	Sophia TANNER
	m	23 Dec 1888	Shasta Co., CA	
	d	6 Sep 1911	Fall River Mills, Shasta Co., CA	
13 John Conrad	b	17 Mar 1858	Des Moines, Polk Co., IA	Addie McNAMER
	m	18 Sep 1887	Pittville, Shasta Co., CA	
	d	10 Jun 1934	Pt. Angeles, Clallam Co., WA	
14 Israel Sloan	b	9 Jun 1860	on the Oregontrail, Neb. Terr.	—
	m	—	never married	
	d	13 Jan 1937	Fall River Mills, Shasta Co., CA	
15 Lucy Priscilla	b	25 Jul 1862	Paradise, Stanislaus Co., CA	John W. CHILDERS
	m	3 Oct 1878	Los Banos, Merced Co., CA	
	d	?	?	

References   Itemize each source used to document names, dates, and places for each member of the family

Page/Source	Type of Record	In Reference To	Information Given
IN 3	History	Jesse	Father of John
IN 11	1840 Census	John	4 males, 2 females
IN 42	1850 Census	John & family	John, 35, Lucy 28 + 6 children + Philip REYNOLDS
IN 54	Marriage Rec'd	John & Lucy	date, place
IN 71	Deed Record	John & Lucy	date 1852 in Jasper Co IN
IA 32	1846 IA Terr. Census	John & family	2 males, 3 females
IA 34	History	John	mentioned as United Brethren minister
IA 59	1854 IA State Census	John	4 males, 4 females
CA 3	1866 Voter's Reg.	John	1866, age 51, b. IN, peddler. Yolo Co CA
CA 3	1869 " "	John	1869 Stanislaus Co CA
CA 4	Cemetery Rec'd	Mary	m Miles TANNER.
CA 13	1900 Census CA	John C. & fam	
CA 13	1900 CA Census	Samuel W.	living w/ John C. & family.
CA 18	History	Israel	stage driver
CA 20	Death Cert.	Israel	b. d.
CA 21	Marriage Rec'd	John C. & Addie	J.C. age 29, b. IA, Adda, 18 b. CA
CA 27	1900 CA Census	Israel	b. 1860, boarder.
CA 27	Photograph	"	
CA 31	Obituary	Israel	1937
CA 32	Obituary	Samuel	1909
CA 39	Index to deaths	Samuel, Israel	1937, 1909
CA 40	1870 CA Census	Lucy & fam	Lucy age 42, w/ Samuel, Lawrence, John, Lucy, Israel
CA 41	1870 Mortality	John	d. Dec 1869 age 56 b. IN
CA 42	Personal Accounts	John C., Albert	by A.P., interviewed 1975
CA 43	Marriage	Lucy P.	to John Childers
CA 45	Cemetery	Nancy	m SA SMITH d. 1879
CA 46	History	"	mentioned, wife of Samuel Smith
CA 47	Wm. H.H	Voter's Reg.	1871, age 26, b IN
CA 47	Lawrence	" "	1877, age 21 b. CA, res Los Banos
CA 58	"	Death Cert.	b. d. parents
CA 59	Sophia	" "	wife of Lawrence.
CA 63	Samuel W.	" "	b. d. parents
CA 81	Mary	Cemetery	wife of Miles TANNER. d. 1910 age 47
CA 82	John, Lucy & Fam	Family Bible	births, deaths, marriages
CA 85	Mary	Obituary	d. 1910, Plumas Co CA
CA 86	Mary	Death Cert.	b. d. parents

Family Group Sheet Continuation Sheet. (9 thru 15 children). This form is designed to be used with the Family Group Sheet which has up to 8 children. This sheet can be printed to the backside of the first form, or used as another one-sided sheet.

Continuation, Family of

Children (continued)		DAY MONTH YEAR	PLACE OF EVENT	NAME OF SPOUSE (s)
9	b			
	m			
	d			
10	b			
	m			
	d			
11	b			
	m			
	d			
12	b			
	m			
	d			
13	b			
	m			
	d			
14	b			
	m			
	d			
15	b			
	m			
	d			
16	b			
	m			
	d			
17	b			
	m			
	d			
18	b			
	m			
	d			

References   Itemize each source used to document names, dates, and places for each member of the family

Page/Source	Type of Record	In Reference To	Information Given

Continuation, Family of _Rev. John and Lucy (REYNOLDS) DOLLARHIDE_

Children (continued)		DAY MONTH YEAR	PLACE OF EVENT	NAME OF SPOUSE (s)
9 Merinda	b	9 Apr 1851	Jasper Co., IN	—
	m	—	—	
	d	25 Aug 1851	Jasper Co., IN	
10 Samuel Walker	b	28 Aug 1852	Illinois	—
	m	—	never married	
	d	18 Sep 1909	Fall River Mills, Shasta Co., CA	
11 Loretta Lucy	b	21 Feb 1854	Illinois	David S. KEENER
	m	5 May 1870	Butte Co., CA	
	d	27 Mar 1929	Oroville, Butte Co., CA	
12 Lawrence	b	9 Apr 1856	Fayette Co., IA	Sophia TANNER
	m	23 Dec 1885	Shasta Co., CA	
	d	6 Sep 1911	Fall River Mills, Shasta Co., CA	
13 John Conrad	b	17 Mar 1858	Des Moines, Polk Co., IA	Addie McNAMER
	m	18 Sept 1887	Pittville, Shasta Co., CA	
	d	10 Jan 1934	Pt. Angeles, Clallam Co., WA	
14 Israel Sloan	b	9 Jun 1860	on the Oregon Trail, Neb. Terr.	—
	m	—	never married	
	d	13 Jan 1937	Fall River Mills, Shasta Co., CA	
15 Lucy Priscilla	b	25 Jul 1862	Paradise, Stanislaus Co., CA	John W. CHILDERS
	m	3 Oct 1878	Los Banos, Merced Co., CA	
	d	?	?	
16 Infant	b	stillborn 1863	Paradise, Stanislaus Co., CA	—
	m	—	—	
	d	stillborn 1863	Paradise, Stanislaus Co., CA	
17	b			
	m			
	d			
18	b			
	m			
	d			

References   Itemize each source used to document names, dates, and places for each member of the family

Page/Source	Type of Record	In Reference To	Information Given
IN 3	History	Jesse	Father of John
IN 11	1840 IN Census	John	4 males, 2 females
IN 42	1850 IN Census	John & Family	John, 35; Lucy, 28; plus 6 children
IN 54	Marriage Recd	John & Lucy	date, place
IN 71	Deed Record	John & Lucy	1852 in Jasper Co IN
IA 32	1846 IA Terr. Census	John & Family	2 males, 3 females
IA 59	1854 IA St. Census	John	4 males, 4 females
IA 34	History	John	United Brethren minister
CA 3	1866 Voter's Regis.	John	age 51 in 1866, b. IN, peddler, Yolo Co CA
CA 3	1869 "	"	Stanislaus Co., CA
CA 11	Cemetery Recd	Mary	m. Mike TANNER, hsd b. d.
CA 13	1900 Ch Census	John C. & Fam.	age, nativity
CA 13	" " "	Samuel W.	living w/ John C. & Fam.
CA 18	History	Israel	mentioned as stage driver

Family Group Sheet Continuation Sheet. (9 thru 18 children). This form is designed to be used with the Family Group Sheet which has up to 8 children. This sheet can be printed to the backside of the first form, or used as another one-sided sheet.

Continuation, Family of _____

References (continued)

Page / Source	Type of Record	In Reference to	Information Given

Continuation, Family of *Rev. John and Lucy (REYNOLDS) DOLLARHIDE*

References (continued)

Page / Source	Type of Record	In Reference to	Information Given
CA-20	Death cert.	Israel	birth, death dates, parents
CA-21	Marriage Record	John C. & Addie	J.C., age 21 b. IA, Addie, 18, b. CA
CA-27	1900 CA Census	Israel	b. 1860, boarder
CA-27	photograph	"	
CA-31	Obituary	Israel	1937
CA-32	Obituary	Samuel	1909
CA-3A	Index to deaths	Samuel, Israel	CA st. deaths
CA-40	1870 CA Census	Lucy & fam.	Lucy, age 49 w/Samuel, Lawrence, John C., Israel, & Lucy
CA-41	1870 Mortality	John	d. Dec 1869, age 52, b. IN
CA-42	Personal Accounts	John C., Albert	by Albert R., interviewed 1975
CA-43	Marriage	Lucy P	to John childish
CA-45	Cemetery	Nancy	m. Samuel SMITH, buried 1879
CA-46	History	"	mentioned, wife of Samuel SMITH
CA-47	William H.H.	Voter's Reg.	1871, age 26, b. IN
CA-47	Lawrence	"	1877, age 21, b. CA, res. Los Banos, CA
CA-58	"	Death Cert.	birth, death, parents
CA-59	Sophia	" "	wife of Lawrence
CA-63	Samuel W.	" "	birth, death, parents
CA-61	Mary	Cemetery	wife of Miles TENNER, d. 1911, age 67
CA-82	John, Lucy & fam.	Family Bible	births, deaths, marriages, all 15 children
CA-85	Mary	Obituary	d. 1910, Plumas Co. CA
CA-86	Mary	Death Cert.	birth, death, parents
CA-96	1880 CA Census	Lucy & fam.	Lucy, age 60, w/ Samuel, Lawrence, Israel, Loretta
CA-96	Voter's Reg.	Samuel W.	age 27, 1880, Butte Co CA
CA-96	" "	Lawrence	age 24, 1880, " " "
CA-96	" "	Lawrence	1890, Butte Co CA
CA-96	" "	Lawrence	1892, Butte Co CA, phys. description
CA-98	Newspaper Article	Nancy	S. Smith family in Los Banos, CA
CA-126	Death Record	Lucy	"Lucene" d. 1892, Butte Co CA

Family Group Sheet — References This form is designed to be used with the Family Group Sheet, adding space for more itemized references for a particular family. This sheet can be printed to the backside of the first form, or used as another one-sided sheet.

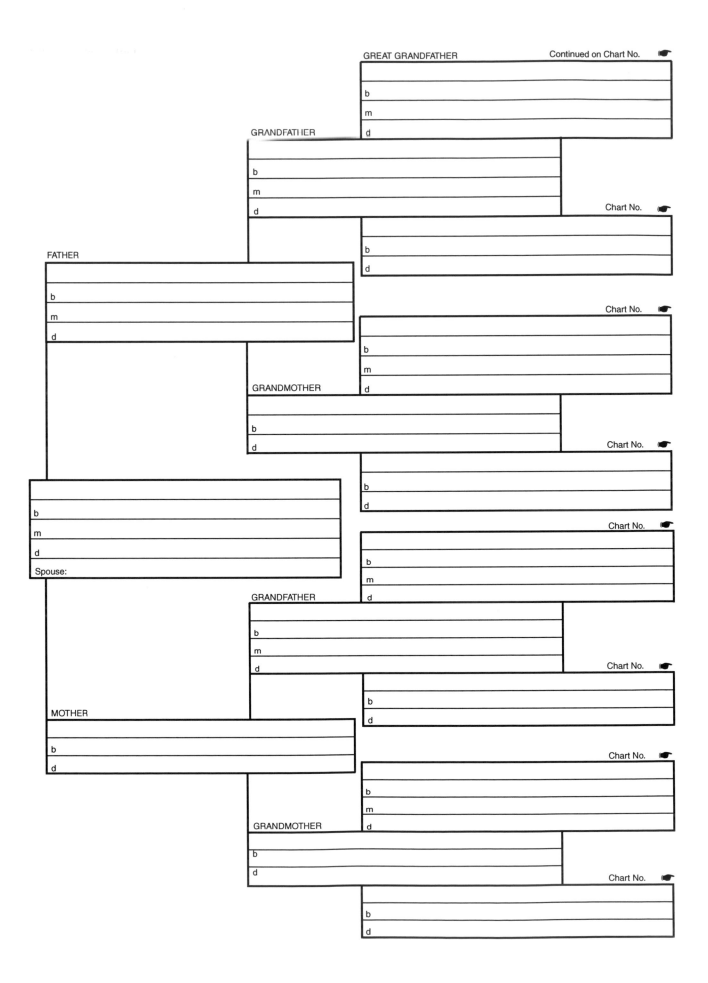

GREAT GRANDFATHER

Continued on Chart No.

b

m

d

GRANDFATHER

b

m

d

Chart No.

b

d

FATHER

b

m

d

Chart No.

b

m

d

GRANDMOTHER

b

d

Chart No.

b

d

b

m

d

Spouse:

Chart No.

b

m

d

GRANDFATHER

b

m

d

Chart No.

b

d

MOTHER

b

d

Chart No.

b

m

d

GRANDMOTHER

b

d

Chart No.

b

d

Pedigree Chart

Chart No. _1_

FATHER

2. Albert Raymond DOLLARHIDE
b 19 Apr 1905, Oakland, Douglas Co., OR
m 30 Jan 1930, Puyallup, Pierce Co., WA
d 18 Mar 1977, Blaine, Whatcom Co., WA

1. William Wiles DOLLARHIDE
b 17 Apr 1942, Seattle, King Co., WA
m (1) 6 Oct 1967, Carson City, NV
  lives in Salt Lake City, UT
spouse: (1) Mary E. SMITH, (2) Linda K. LAWSON

MOTHER

3. Marjory Watkins WILES
b 28 Mar 1906, St. Joseph, Buchanan Co., MO
d 15 Oct 1996, Blaine, Whatcom Co., WA

Prepared By:
William Dollarhide
Salt Lake City, UT

GRANDFATHER

4. John Conrad DOLLARHIDE
b 17 Mar 1858, Des Moines, Polk Co., IA
m 18 Sep 1887, Pittville, Shasta Co., CA
d 7 Jun 1934, Pt. Angeles, Clallam Co., WA

GRANDMOTHER

5. Addie McNEMAR
b 20 Mar 1869, Salem, Marion Co., OR
d 19 Feb 1944, Seattle, King Co., WA

GRANDFATHER

6. Elmer Ross WILES
b 25 Jul 1876, Afton, Union Co., IA
m 14 Jun 1905, Independence, Montgomery Co., KS
d 3 Feb 1953, Seattle, King Co., WA

GRANDMOTHER

7. Julia Angeline WATKINS
b 7 Dec 1882, McFall, Gentry Co., MO
d 3 Feb 1962, Seattle, King Co., WA

GREAT GRANDFATHER   Continued on Chart No. *8* ☞

8. Rev. John DOLLARHIDE
b 1 Nov 1814, Harrison Twp., Wayne Co., IN
m 3 Mar 1836, Tippecanoe Co., IN
d 22 Dec 1869, Lodi, San Joaquin Co., CA

Chart No. *9* ☞

9. Lucy Ann REYNOLDS
b 25 Dec 1820, Troy, Miami Co., OH
d 22 Nov 1892, Dayton, Butte Co., CA

Chart No. *10* ☞

10. John Hurley McNEMAR
b 20 Mar 1848, Louisa Co., IA
m 9 Mar 1868, Vancouver, Clark Co., WA Terr.
d 22 Jan 1922, Forest Grove, Wash. Co., OR

Chart No. *11* ☞

11. Amanda Jane MAYFIELD
b 24 Aug 1852, Des Moines, Polk Co., IA
d 27 Apr 1931, Pt. Angeles, Clallam Co., WA

12. David H. WILES
b 7 Nov 1845, Rochester, Fulton Co., IN
m 29 Nov 1868, Afton, Union Co., IA
d 3 Sep 1935, Sheridan, Sheridan Co., WY

Chart No. *13* ☞

13. Susan Jane NEEDHAM
b 10 Sep 1849, Marion, Grant Co., IN
d 15 Jun 1932, Sheridan, Sheridan Co., WY

Chart No. *14* ☞

14. Benjamin Abijah WATKINS
b 6 Jan 1842, Boon(e), Warrick Co., IN
m about 1873 in Gentry Co., MO (?)
d 22 Dec 1914, Edna, Labette Co., KS

Chart No. *15* ☞

15. Miranda BLACK
b 18 Mar 1839, Indiana
d 27 Aug 1892, Davies Co. (?) MO

Pedigree Chart. This form is for identifying the direct ancestors of one person. The first person should be given the number 1. That person's father should be number 2. All males should be in an upper position and have an even number. All females are in a lower position and have an odd number.

4.	John Conrad DOLLARHIDE
	b. 17 Mar 1858, Des Moines, IA
	m. 18 Sep 188_, Pittville, Shasta Co., CA
	d. 7 Jun 1934, Pt. Angeles, WA
	bur. Oceanview Cemetery, Port Angeles, WA
5.	Addie McNEMAR
	b. 20 Mar 1869, Salem, OR
	d. 17 Feb 1944, Seattle, WA
	bur. Oceanview Cemetery, Port Angeles, WA
6.	Elmer Ross WILES
	b. 25 Jul 1876, Afton, Union Co., IA
	m. 14 Jun 1905, Independence, Montgomery Co., IA
	d. 3 Feb 1953, Seattle, WA
	bur. Crown Hill Cemetery, Seattle, WA
7.	Julia Angeline WATKINS
	b. 9 Dec 1882, McFall, Gentry Co., MO
	d. 3 Feb 1942, Seattle, WA
	bur. Crown Hill Cemetery, Seattle, WA
8.	Rev. John DOLLARHIDE
	b. 1 Nov 1814, Wayne Co., IN
	m. 3 Mar 1836, Tippecanoe Co., IN
	d. 22 Dec 1869, Lodi, CA
9.	Lucy Ann Reynolds
	b. 25 Dec 1810, Miami Co., OH
	d. 22 Nov 1872, Dayton, CA
10.	John Hurley McNEMAR
	b. 20 Mar 1849, Louisa Co., IA
	m. 9 Mar 1868, Vancouver, WA Ter.
	d. 12 Jan 1922, Forest Grove, OR
11.	Amanda Jane MAYFIELD
	b. 24 Aug 1852, Des Moines, IA
	d. 27 Apr 1934, Pt. Angeles, WA
12.	David H. WILES
	b. 7 Nov 1845, Fulton Co., IN
	m. 29 Nov 1868, Union Co., IA
	d. 3 Sep 1935, Sheridan, WY
13.	Susan Jane NEEDHAM
	b. 10 Sep 1849, Grant Co., IN
	d. 15 Jun 1932, Sheridan, WY
14.	Benjamin Abijah WATKINS
	b. 6 Jan 1842, Warrick Co., IN
	m. 1873, Gentry Co. (?) MO
	d. 22 Dec 1914, Edna, KS
15.	Miranda BLACK
	b. 18 Mar 1831, Indiana
	d. 27 Aug 1897, Missouri
16.	Jesse DOLLARHIDE
	b. abt 1785, NC; d. 22 Dec 1840, IN
17.	Nancy Jane PIERSON
	b. abt 1794 KY; d. 1878, Iowa
18.	Philip REYNOLDS
	b. 1788 VA, d. 1878 OR
19.	Sophia HILL b. 1795-1796 in VA; d. ca 1845, Tippecanoe Co. IN
20.	Noah Wheeler McNEMAR
	b. 1816 in OH; d. 1854 in OR
21.	Margaret HURLEY
	b. abt 1818 in OH; d. 1848 in IA
22.	James Henry MAYFIELD
	b. 1828 in TN; d. after 1910 CA?
23.	Tobiatha OSBORNE
	b. 1828 in TN; d. before 1900 CA? OR?
24.	William WILES
	b. 1822 in PA; d. 1878 in TX
25.	Nancy Jane RUMBAUGH
	b. 1822 in PA; d. 1911 in IA
26.	John NEEDHAM
	b. 1822 in IN; d. 1905 in IA
27.	Mary WINSLOW
	b. 1824 in NC; d. 1915 in CA
28.	Abijah WATKINS
	b. abt 1800 in KY(?); d.? IN
29.	Emily HUFFMAN
	b. abt 1800 in KY; d.? IN
30.	Alexander BLACK
	b. abt 1787 bt in KY; d? IN?
31.	Ann MENIX
	b. abt 1790 in KY; d? IN?

2. Albert Raymond DOLLARHIDE	3. Marjory Watkins WILES
b. 14 Apr 1905, Oakland, Douglas Co., OR	b. 28 Mar 1906, St. Joseph, Buchanan Co., MO
m. 30 Jan 1930, Puyallup, Pierce Co., WA	d. 15 Oct 1996, Blaine, Whatcom Co., WA
d. 18 Mar 1977, Blaine, Whatcom Co., WA	bur. Crown Hill Cemetery, Seattle, WA
bur. Crown Hill Cemetery, Seattle, WA	

1. William Wiles DOLLARHIDE b. 17 Apr 1942, Seattle, King Co., WA
m. 1) Mary Erlene (SMITH) PIPITONE, 6 Oct 1967, Carson City, NV
m. 2) Linda K. LAWSON, 20 Aug 1988, Bellingham, Whatcom Co., WA
lives in Salt Lake City

Pedigree Chart. This form is for identifying the direct ancestors of one person. The first person should be given the number 1. That person's father should be number 2. All males should be in an upper position and have an even number. All females are in a lower position and have an odd number.

Ancestor Table   Surname: Table No.

	m date
b	
d	m place
b	m date
d	m place
b	m date
d	m place
b	m date
d	m place
b	m date
d	m place
b	m date
d	m place
b	m date
d	m place
b	m date
d	m place
b	m date
d	m place
b	m date
d	m place
b	m date
d	m place
b	m date
d	m place
b	m date
d	m place

Ancestor Table	Surname: *DOLLARHIDE*	Table No. *1*

1. William Wiles DOLLARHIDE	m 1) Mary (SMITH) PIPITONE ; m 2) Linda K. LAWSON
b 17 Apr 1942, Seattle, King Co., WA	m date 1) 6 Oct 1967, Carson City, NV
d –	m place 2) 20 Aug 1988, Bellingham, WA
2. Albert Raymond DOLLARHIDE	3. Marjory Watkins WILES
b 14 Apr 1905, Oakland, Douglas Co., OR	m date 18 Jan 1930
d 18 Mar 1977, Blaine, Whatcom Co., WA	m place Puyallup, Pierce Co., WA
4. John Conrad DOLLARHIDE	5. Addie McNAMER
b 17 Mar 1858, Des Moines, Polk Co., IA	m date 18 Sep 1887
d 7 Jan 1934, Pt. Angeles, Clallam Co., CA	m place Pittville, Shasta Co., CA
8. Rev. John DOLLARHIDE	9. Lucy REYNOLDS
b 1 Nov 1814, Wayne Co., IN	m date 3 Mar 1836
d 22 Dec 1869, Lodi, San Joaquin Co., CA	m place Tippecanoe Co., IN
16. Jesse DOLLARHIDE	17. Nancy PIERSON
b abt 1785 in North Carolina	m date 11 Nov 1813
d 22 Feb 1840, Tippecanoe Co., IN	m place Preble Co., OH
32. John DOLLARHIDE	33. Nancy Chittington
b 1750 Orange Co., NC	m date 3 Nov 1784
d 1851, Lufkin, Angelina Co., TX	m place Caswell Co., NC
64. Francis DOLLAHIDE, III	65. — —
b before 1623, Baltimore Co., MD	m date abt 1744, Baltimore Co., MD
d before 1740, Randolph Co., NC	m place MD
128. Francis DOLLAHIDE, Jr.	129. Mary (CALLMACK) BRADSHAW
b about 1700 in Baltimore Co., MD	m date about 1721 in Baltimore Co., MD
d before 1738 in Baltimore Co., MD	m place MD
256. Francis DOLLAHIDE, Sr.	251. Providence TOLLEY
b about 1655, County Dublin, Ireland	m date about 1687
d after 20 Oct 1720, Baltimore Co., MD	m place Ann Arundel Co., MD
512. Andrew DOLLAHIDE	513. — —
b about 1620, Co. Dublin, Ireland	m date abt 1640-50, Co. Dublin, Ireland
d about 1678, Co. Dublin, Ireland	m place
b	m date
d	m place
b	m date
d	m place
b	m date
d	m place

Ancestor Table This form is for identifying a direct line of male ancestors of the same surname. Except for number 1 who could be male or female, the first person identified is always a female. The father of that person is shown next, then his father, grandfather, great-grandfather, and so on. This is another way of looking at a pedigree.

Correspondence Log   Researcher: _____

ITEM NO.	DATE MAILED	CHECK NO.	SUBJECT	REPLY Results - Action - Notes
				Date
Sent To				
				Date
Sent To				
				Date
Sent To				
				Date
Sent To				
				Date
Sent To				
				Date
Sent To				
				Date
Sent To				
				Date
Sent To				
				Date
Sent To				

Correspondence Log   Researcher: _William Dollarhide_

ITEM NO.	DATE MAILED	CHECK NO.	SUBJECT	REPLY Results - Action - Notes
121	2/8/98	—	reply to his letter. He sent	Date
Sent To _Ralph Henderson_			NEEDHAM/JENNINGS data.	No action req'd
2052 B. Bobcat				
Langley AFB, VA 23665				
122	2/9/98	$4.00 921	answered ad in Helper.	Date 2/17/98
Sent To _Anundsen Publishing Co_			Sent for "Your Manuscript	rec'd booklet. see file cab.
108 Washington			in Print"	"printers"
Decorah, IA 52101				
123	2/9/98	—	Research in NC Archives	Date 2/24/98
Sent To _Jonathan Butcher_			Asked for info, fees, etc.	rec'd letter
Box 531			SASE	
Cary, NC 27511				
124	2/9/80	$22/ $2.00	Sent for guide to PA	Date 3/1/98
Sent To _S.W. PA Gen'l Services_			sources, "The Pennsylvania	Rec'd booklet. See States File-PA
PO Box 253E			Line"	
Laughlintown, PA 15655				
125	2/12/98	—	Sent for application for	Date 2/25/98 $4.50/yr dues.
Sent To _Randolph Co IN G.S._			membership. Asked for	2 cemetery (index cards) rec'ds.
% Monica Wiseman, Rte 3,			surname check, DOLLARHIDE,	(See RFDS IN 43)
Winchester, IN 47394			in Randolph Co IN	
126	2/12/98	—	Sent for info & samples	Date 2/8/98 — rec'd material.
Sent To _Personalized Computer_			of genealogical computer files,	not impressed.
Service, 1700 Baywood Dr #303			indexing, etc.	
Bay City, TX 77414				
127	3/8/98	—	Sent info on Philip McNEMAR	Date Rec'd letter. Good info!
Sent To _Wayne McNAMER_			of Ross Co. OH 1796-1820.	Sent copy of Philip Reynold's will!
Box 565, Lucasville, OH			Can he connect?	Gives son, "Noah",
_45648_				(See RFDS OH 21)
128	5/1/98	$50.00 1044	Sent details re Dollarhide	Date 6/1/98 rec'd report.
Sent To _Jonathan Butcher_			in Randolph Co NC	Good info! (See RFDS NC 60-72)
(see 123)				
129	6/1/68	—	Sent info on Francis	Date 6/12/98 rec'd letter, w/votes
Sent To _Anna Cartlidge_			Dollarhide in MD. Asked	sound check.
362 E. Belvedere Ave.			for votes.	
Baltimore MD 21212				

Correspondence Log. This form is for keeping track of letters mailed in a genealogical project, logging letters or E-mails requesting information from various agencies, money sent out, or letters to other genealogists. By reviewing the log entries from time to time, a researcher has a reminder of work that has been done, an indication of letters that have gone unanswered, and follow-up work that may be necessary.

Research Journal

Researcher:

DATE	ACTIVITY	RESULTS

Research Journal		Researcher: *William Dollahide*
DATE	ACTIVITY	RESULTS
4/3/79	Several hours spent looking through the MARYLAND ARCHIVES volumes at the Hall of Records, Annapolis, MD. In search of Francis DOLLAHIDE, member of the Legislative Assembly, Colonial Maryland, 1701-1722	Vol. nothing Vol 2+3 Not avail Vol. 4 nothing Vol. 5, 6, +7 nothing Vol. 8 +9 not avail. Vol. 10 nothing Vol. 11 not avail.
	Vol. 26: Francis DOLLAHYDE, in House Of Delegates. See pp. 48, 63, 64, 74, 77, 99, 104, 120, 132, 148, 164, 185, 207, 377, 380, 382, 389, 401, 403, 457, 476, 482, 493, 501, 532, 533, 543, 548, 550, 561, 579, 580, 599, 606, 610, 618, and 638.	Vol. 12 nothing Vol. 14 not avail. Vol. 15/16 nothing Vol. 17/18 not avail. Vol. 19 thru 25 nothing Vol. 26. See RFDS shts Vol. 28 Nothing Vol. 29 " Vol. 30 See RFDS shts Vol. 31, 32 Nothing
	Vol. 27: Francis DOLLAHYDE pp 61, 66. p.61: "at general assembly for the province of Maryland... 26 Mar. 1707" p. 66: Francis, commissioned to serve in the office of High sherriff of Balto Co MD	Vol. 33 See RFDS shts Vol. 34 See RFDS shts Vol. 35: nothing Vol. 36-37 nothing
	Vol. 30: Francis DOLLAHIDE. See pp 64, 71, 85, 87, 89, 95, 107, 160, 162, 176, 190, 219, 360, 477, 479, 481, 515, 554, 556, 573, 574, and 582.	
	Vol. 33 Fr. Dollahide. See pp 54, 70, 201, 220, 227, 255, 271, 365, 386, 505, 507, 565, 592, and 594.	
	Vol. 34: "Capt Frd. DALLAHDE" member from Balto Co MD. Session began 22 Apr 1720 p. 204: "Capt. DOLLAHDE, deceased"	←See RFDS MD 47 he died between sessions ending 28 Apr 1720 and renewed July 1721.
4/4/79	Continuing w/ Maryland Archives Vol. 31: p5, 59, and 376: John BRADSHAW, petition sent to Lower House, 1732.	

Research Journal. This form is for keeping track of research tasks that have been undertaken with an indication of the success. This is a method of recording steps taken, books and documents reviewed, and searches conducted. Recording research tasks that were unsuccessful may prevent a researcher from repeating the tasks.

Relationship Chart

A relationship between two people can be determined if a common ancestor is known. The two lineages should both begin with the common ancestor, shown on the chart as Number 1. Next, list two lineages, one line shown below as A2, A3, A4, etc., which moves up, and the other as B2, B3, B4, etc., which moves down. By tracing any two persons to a point in the box where the gray or white bands intersect, a legal relationship can be found. For example, A3 and B3 are first cousins, but A3 and B4 are first cousins, once removed.

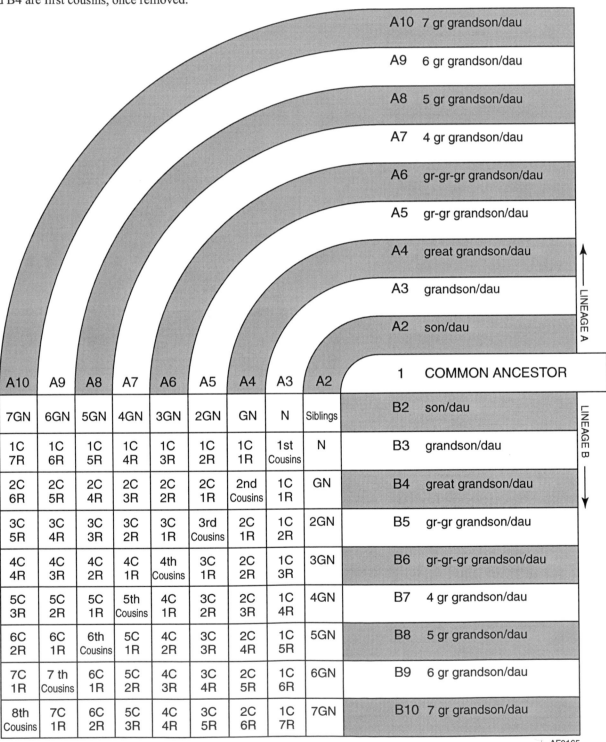

A10	7 gr grandson/dau
A9	6 gr grandson/dau
A8	5 gr grandson/dau
A7	4 gr grandson/dau
A6	gr-gr-gr grandson/dau
A5	gr-gr grandson/dau
A4	great grandson/dau
A3	grandson/dau
A2	son/dau

LINEAGE A

| 1 | COMMON ANCESTOR |

LINEAGE B

A10	A9	A8	A7	A6	A5	A4	A3	A2		
7GN	6GN	5GN	4GN	3GN	2GN	GN	N	Siblings	B2	son/dau
1C 7R	1C 6R	1C 5R	1C 4R	1C 3R	1C 2R	1C 1R	1st Cousins	N	B3	grandson/dau
2C 6R	2C 5R	2C 4R	2C 3R	2C 2R	2C 1R	2nd Cousins	1C 1R	GN	B4	great grandson/dau
3C 5R	3C 4R	3C 3R	3C 2R	3C 1R	3rd Cousins	2C 1R	1C 2R	2GN	B5	gr-gr grandson/dau
4C 4R	4C 3R	4C 2R	4C 1R	4th Cousins	3C 1R	2C 2R	1C 3R	3GN	B6	gr-gr-gr grandson/dau
5C 3R	5C 2R	5C 1R	5th Cousins	4C 1R	3C 2R	2C 3R	1C 4R	4GN	B7	4 gr grandson/dau
6C 2R	6C 1R	6th Cousins	5C 1R	4C 2R	3C 3R	2C 4R	1C 5R	5GN	B8	5 gr grandson/dau
7C 1R	7 th Cousins	6C 1R	5C 2R	4C 3R	3C 4R	2C 5R	1C 6R	6GN	B9	6 gr grandson/dau
8th Cousins	7C 1R	6C 2R	5C 3R	4C 4R	3C 5R	2C 6R	1C 7R	7GN	B10	7 gr grandson/dau

AF0165

Relationship Chart

A relationship between two people can be determined if a common ancestor is known. The two lineages should both begin with the common ancestor, shown on the chart as number 1. Next, list two lineages, one line shown below as A2, A3, A4, etc., which moves up, and the other as B2, B3, B4, etc., which moves down. By tracing any two persons to a point in the box where the grey or white bands intersect, a legal relationship can be found. For example, A3 and B3 are first cousins, but A3 and B4 are first cousins, once removed.

LEGEND:

N = niece or nephew to uncle or aunt.
GN = Great niece or nephew.
2C 1R = second cousins, once removed.
3C 4R = third cousins, four times removed.

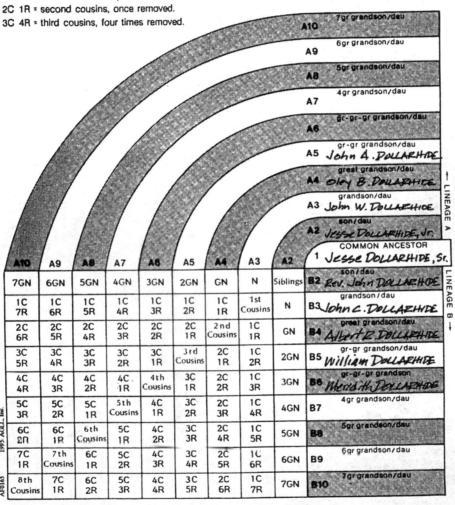

A10	A9	A8	A7	A6	A5	A4	A3	A2	
7GN	6GN	5GN	4GN	3GN	2GN	GN	N	Siblings	**B2** *Rev. John DOLLARHIDE*
1C 7R	1C 6R	1C 5R	1C 4R	1C 3R	1C 2R	1C 1R	1st Cousins	N	**B3** *John C. DOLLARHIDE*
2C 6R	2C 5R	2C 4R	2C 3R	2C 2R	2C 1R	2nd Cousins	1C 1R	GN	**B4** *Albert E. DOLLARHIDE*
3C 5R	3C 4R	3C 3R	3C 2R	3C 1R	3rd Cousins	2C 1R	1C 2R	2GN	**B5** *William DOLLARHIDE*
4C 4R	4C 3R	4C 2R	4C 1R	4th Cousins	3C 1R	2C 2R	1C 3R	3GN	**B6** *Meridith DOLLARHIDE*
5C 3R	5C 2R	5C 1R	5th Cousins	4C 1R	3C 2R	2C 3R	1C 4R	4GN	**B7**
6C 2R	6C 1R	6th Cousins	5C 1R	4C 2R	3C 3R	2C 4R	1C 5R	5GN	**B8**
7C 1R	7th Cousins	6C 1R	5C 2R	4C 3R	3C 4R	2C 5R	1C 6R	6GN	**B9**
8th Cousins	7C 1R	6C 2R	5C 3R	4C 4R	3C 5R	2C 6R	1C 7R	7GN	**B10**

1995 AGLL, Inc.

AF9165

Relationship Chart. Use this chart to determine the relationship between any two persons who share a common ancestor.

Personal/Home Sources

☐ Family Bibles
☐ Oral Histories
☐ Family Histories
☐ Baby Books
☐ Baby Announcements
☐ Wedding Announcements
☐ Wedding Guest Books
☐ Diaries and Journals
☐ Income Tax Forms
☐ Property Tax Receipts
☐ Family Correspondence
☐ Funeral Programs
☐ Death Announcements
☐ Scrapbooks
☐ Photo Albums
☐ Credit Statements
☐ Discharge Papers
☐ Draft Cards
☐ Military Awards
☐ Social Security Cards
☐ Magazine Subscriptions
☐ First Papers - Citizenship
☐ Naturalization Papers
☐ Employment Papers
☐ Union Cards
☐ Newspaper Clippings
☐ Probate/Estate Records
☐ Wills
☐ Land Deeds
☐ Drivers Licenses
☐ Motor Vehicle Registrations
☐ Adoption Record
☐ Baptism Record
☐ Report Cards
☐ School Enrollment
☐ Confirmation Record
☐ Graduation Record
☐ Diploma
☐ Family Fraktur
☐ Family Needlepoint
☐ Prepared Pedigrees
☐ Prepared Descendancies
☐ Prepared Ahnentafels
☐ Birth Certificate
☐ Marriage Certificate
☐ Death Certificate
☐ Death Certificate
☐ Divorce Papers
☐ Life Insurance Papers
☐ Fire Insurance Papers
☐ Automobile Insurance
   Papers
☐ Health Insurance Papers
☐ Misc. Family Records

Vital Records

☐ State Birth Indexes
☐ State Death Indexes
☐ State Marriage Indexes
☐ County Birth Records
☐ County Death Records
☐ County Marriage Records
☐ Birth Certificates
☐ Delayed Birth Certificate
☐ Corrected Birth Certificate
☐ Marriage Bonds
☐ Marriage Licenses
☐ Marriage Certificates
☐ Death Certificates
☐ Divorce Papers
☐ Adoption Papers
☐ Social Security Death Index
☐ Social Security Work History

School Records

☐ Report Cards
☐ Grade School Records
☐ High School Records
☐ Trade School Records
☐ Apprenticeship Records
☐ Private School Records
☐ University Records
☐ School Alumni Records
☐ School Annuals
☐ School Reunion Records
☐ School Newspapers
☐ Attendance Reports
☐ School Awards
☐ Graduation Cards
☐ Class Pictures

Church Records

☐ Birth Records
☐ Christening Records
☐ Baptismal Records
☐ Dedication Records
☐ Confirmation Records
☐ Marriage Banns
☐ Death Records
☐ Burial Records
☐ Vestry Records
☐ Admissions
☐ Removals
☐ Disciplinary Records
☐ Church Minutes
☐ Church Histories
☐ Seminary Records
☐ Church Archives
☐ Annulments
☐ Membership Lists

☐ Minister's Records
☐ Ordination Records
☐ Missionary Records
☐ Misc. Church Records

Newspapers

☐ Newspaper Indexes
☐ Obituaries
☐ Death Notices
☐ Birth Announcements
☐ Marriage Notices
☐ Anniversaries
☐ Milestones
☐ Biographies
☐ Family Stories
☐ Historical Pieces
☐ Unclaimed Mail
☐ Advertisements
☐ Local News
☐ Regional Correspondents
☐ Gossip Columns
☐ Bankruptcies
☐ Sheriff Sales
☐ Divorces
☐ Court Claims
☐ Auctions
☐ Probates
☐ Criminal Convictions
☐ Ship Arrival Notice
☐ Ship Departure Notice

Federal Censuses

☐ 1790 Printed Index
☐ 1790 Schedules
☐ 1800 Printed Index
☐ 1800 Schedules
☐ 1810 Printed Index
☐ 1810 Schedules
☐ 1820 Printed Index
☐ 1820 Schedules
☐ 1830 Printed Index
☐ 1840 Schedules
☐ 1840 Veterans List
☐ 1850 Printed Index
☐ 1850 Schedules
☐ 1850 Slave Schedules
☐ 1850 Mortality Schedules
☐ 1860 Printed Index
☐ 1860 Schedules
☐ 1860 Slave Schedules
☐ 1860 Mortality Schedules
☐ 1870 Printed Index
☐ 1870 Schedules
☐ 1870 Mortality Schedules
☐ 1880 Printed Index

☐ 1880 Schedules
☐ 1880 Mortality Schedules
☐ 1880 Soundex
☐ 1890 Veterans Schedules
☐ 1900 Printed Index
☐ 1900 Schedules
☐ 1900 Soundex
☐ 1910 Printed Index
☐ 1910 Schedules
☐ 1910 Soundex/Miracode
☐ 1920 Printed Index
☐ 1920 Schedules
☐ 1920 Soundex
☐ 1930-2000 Census Search

State & Misc. Censuses

☐ State Census Indexes
☐ State Census Schedules
☐ Agriculture Censuses
☐ Social Statistics
☐ State Military Records
☐ Compiled State Records
☐ Veterans Records

Directories

☐ Phone Books
☐ City Directories
☐ County/Rural Directories
☐ Genealogical Research
   Directory (GRD)
☐ American Genealogical &
   Biographical Index (AGBI)
☐ Business Almanacs
☐ Trade/Business Directories
☐ Funeral Directors Directory
☐ Cemeteries Directory
☐ Who's Who Directories

Computer Data Bases

☐ FHL Card Catalog
☐ FHL IGI Searches
☐ FHL Ancestral File
☐ FHL Pedigree Resource File
☐ FHL Family Register
☐ Social Security Death Index
☐ Everton's Root Cellar
☐ Internet Genealogy Sites
☐ Ft. Wayne Library Catalog
☐ National Veterans
   Cemetery Index
☐ Civil War Photos Index

AF0172

Library Sources

- ❏ DAR Library Indexes
- ❏ Libr. of Congress Indexes
- ❏ Newberry Library Indexes
- ❏ Ft. Wayne Library Search Service
- ❏ Ft. Wayne Library PerSI
- ❏ State Library Bio Indexes
- ❏ Local Library Bio Indexes
- ❏ Gen. Society Bio Indexes
- ❏ Annual Periodical Indexes
- ❏ Queries Indexes
- ❏ Indexed Genealogies
- ❏ Historical Articles
- ❏ Name Lists
- ❏ Source Extracts
- ❏ Family Histories
- ❏ County Histories
- ❏ Local Histories

Land Records

- ❏ Land Ownership Atlases
- ❏ Land Ownership Maps
- ❏ Gazetteers
- ❏ Grantee/Grantor Indexes
- ❏ Deeds
- ❏ Mortgages
- ❏ Plats & Tracts
- ❏ Homesteads
- ❏ Land Entry Files
- ❏ Patents
- ❏ Land Surveys
- ❏ Land Grants
- ❏ Land Warrants
- ❏ Land Claims

Court Records

- ❏ Marriage Banns
- ❏ Marriage Bonds
- ❏ Poll Tax Lists
- ❏ Property Tax Lists
- ❏ School Tax Lists
- ❏ Tax Exemptions
- ❏ Business Licenses
- ❏ Professional Registrations
- ❏ Certifications
- ❏ Appointments
- ❏ Sheriff Sales
- ❏ Arrest Records
- ❏ Coroner Records
- ❏ Medical Exam. Reports
- ❏ Jury Lists
- ❏ Brands & Cattle Markings
- ❏ Justice of Peace Records
- ❏ Probate Court Records
- ❏ Testate & Intestate Papers

- ❏ Guardianships
- ❏ Orphan's Court Records
- ❏ Civil Court Records
- ❏ Wills
- ❏ Administrations
- ❏ Case Files
- ❏ Dockets
- ❏ Minutes
- ❏ Judgments
- ❏ Indexes
- ❏ Voter Registrations
- ❏ Legal Name Changes
- ❏ Indentures
- ❏ Insolvents Hearings
- ❏ Bankruptcy Records
- ❏ Lunacy Hearings
- ❏ Court Appeals
- ❏ Executions
- ❏ Stays
- ❏ Foreclosures
- ❏ Injunctions
- ❏ Pleas
- ❏ Depositions
- ❏ Testimonies
- ❏ Declarations
- ❏ Receipts
- ❏ Allegations
- ❏ Examinations
- ❏ Complaints
- ❏ Promissory Notes
- ❏ Estate Inventories
- ❏ Estate Appraisals
- ❏ Arbitrations
- ❏ Bonds
- ❏ Misc. Court Records

Immigration Records

- ❏ Ship Passenger Lists
- ❏ Vaccinations
- ❏ Alien Registrations
- ❏ Oaths of Allegiance
- ❏ Declarations of Intents
- ❏ Naturalization Records
- ❏ Court Minute Books

Cemetery Records

- ❏ Sexton's Records
- ❏ Tombstones
- ❏ Plats & Maps
- ❏ Memorials
- ❏ Gifts
- ❏ Cremation Lists
- ❏ Burial Lists

Mortuary Records

- ❏ Burial Records

- ❏ Funeral Cards
- ❏ Funeral Record Books
- ❏ Transfer Permits
- ❏ Obituaries
- ❏ Financial Statements

Military Records

- ❏ Service Records
- ❏ Pension Records
- ❏ Pensioners Censuses
- ❏ Troop Returns
- ❏ Muster-in Rolls
- ❏ Muster-out Rolls
- ❏ Paymaster Records
- ❏ Inventories
- ❏ Quartermaster Rolls
- ❏ Drill Rolls
- ❏ Desertions
- ❏ Prisoners
- ❏ Dead Rolls
- ❏ List of Recruits
- ❏ Casualty Lists
- ❏ Claims
- ❏ Battle Reports
- ❏ Court Martial Records
- ❏ Military Hospital Records
- ❏ Military Prison Records
- ❏ Officer's Commissions
- ❏ Disabled Veteran Records
- ❏ Bounty Warrants
- ❏ Discharges
- ❏ Military Burial Records
- ❏ Newspaper Military Lists
- ❏ Veteran Admin. Files
- ❏ Service Organization Files
- ❏ Military Unit Reunion Records
- ❏ Military Unit Memorials
- ❏ National Cemetery Indexes
- ❏ Applications for Mil. Burials

State-wide Records

- ❏ State Military Rosters
- ❏ State Vital Statistics Lists
- ❏ State Genealogical Indexes
- ❏ State Biographical Indexes
- ❏ Family Bible Repositories
- ❏ Misc. Surname Files
- ❏ Motor Vehicle Registrations
- ❏ Drivers Licenses
- ❏ Driving Records
- ❏ Professional Licenses
- ❏ Business Licenses
- ❏ Burial Permits & Transfers
- ❏ State Orphanage Records
- ❏ State Employee Records

- ❏ State Hospital Records

Employment Records

- ❏ Union Membership Lists
- ❏ Business Newsletters
- ❏ Apprentices
- ❏ Licenses
- ❏ Pensions
- ❏ Service Awards
- ❏ Personnel Files
- ❏ Account Book
- ❏ Corporate Records
- ❏ Pharmacist Records
- ❏ Local Retail Accounts

Government & Institutions

- ❏ Nursing Home Records
- ❏ Prison Records
- ❏ State Hospitals
- ❏ Private Hospitals
- ❏ Doctor's Medical Records
- ❏ Charitable Organizations
- ❏ Veteran's Organizations
- ❏ Historical Societies
- ❏ Genealogical Societies
- ❏ Orphan Societies
- ❏ Reunion Registries
- ❏ Adoption Registries
- ❏ Private Libraries
- ❏ Museums
- ❏ Interpretive Centers
- ❏ National Parks
- ❏ Patent Applications
- ❏ WWII Internment Records
- ❏ Visa Applications
- ❏ Passport Applications
- ❏ Lighthouse Logbooks
- ❏ Federal Pardon Case Files
- ❏ Railroad Retirements
- ❏ Policeman's Retirements
- ❏ Federal Retirement Records
- ❏ Social Security Work History
- ❏ Social Security Form SS-5
- ❏ Credit Reporting Agencies
- ❏ Private Investigators

Special Collections

- ❏ Indexes
- ❏ Personal Papers
- ❏ Surname Files
- ❏ Biographies
- ❏ DAR Lists
- ❏ Draper Papers
- ❏ Oral History Projects
- ❏ WPA History Projects

Index

All Subheadings in Alphabetical order

Index